RIGHT PL
WRONG

CW00566130

To Carole

Best Wishes

Mick Ritchie

x

RIGHT PLACE...
WRONG TIME

Mark Ritchie

DESERT ♥ HEARTS

First published
in 2020 by
DESERT♥HEARTS
www.deserthearts.com

www.mark-ritchie.co.uk

www.ukcabaret.com

Typeset and designed by Desert♥Hearts

Printed and bound in Great Britain by
Printforce

British Library Cataloguing in Publication Data
A catalogue record for this book is available from the British Library

ISBN 9781908755438

**

This book is dedicated to
Tommy Brooks
and to
Lassie, Barney, Oscar,
Stan & Ollie

"I'll stay until the end – Like any other dinosaur.
Until I'm phased out – As everyone is eventually,
when they finally outlive their usefulness . . ."

—1—

Up until the age of about ten there really was nothing remarkable about my life, my family life or my upbringing. On January 21st 2020, I was 61 years old – and I thought it was about time to cough this story up, like a cat with a furball.

I had originally planned to write about the history of the UK working men's club movement. Then quite by chance I met the former magazine editor and critic Robert Gore Langton, who read through my first draft and declared that in his opinion the most interesting bits were those concerning my own life.

It never occurred to me that my little life was so out of the ordinary. When you are the one actually living the life, you just get on with it I suppose. Call it lack of self-awareness. Call it stoicism. Whatever the reason, a light came on in my head and I realised what I had actually lived through. The places I had been and worked. The people I'd met. The mix of experiences.

I have apparently lived through a social revolution, and serendipity has clearly been conjuring its magic to keep me out of too much trouble despite being in the wrong place at the wrong time for most of my life.

Life is full of potential banana-skins. In show business the brickbats and bouquets come thick and fast. What follows is the life I have lived. No lies and nothing held back. This is me and some stories of my life.

My life experience began in a dormitory mining village in Yorkshire, where I was born on January 21st 1959, the third child of my parents Frank and Mavis. A brother Steven Edward Goodwin had died as a baby from meningitis. My sister Barbara is six years older than me and then there was me. Born in the front bedroom of 29 Mill Lane in the village of Ryhill on a Thursday, in the late afternoon/early evening.

Monday's child is fair of face
Tuesday's child is full of grace
Wednesday's child is full of woe
Thursday's child has far to go
Friday's child is loving and giving
Saturday's child works hard for his living.
And the child that is born on the Sabbath day, is
*   bonny and blithe and good and gay.*

So according to the story of pantomime heroine Mother Goose, I had 'far to go'. I have certainly gone far, but seldom taking the optimum route.

*

The rented house in Mill Lane where I was born was almost exactly across the road from the home of my paternal grandparents Albert Webster Goodwin and his wife, my grandmother Mabel. They lived in the house that my dad and his three older sisters Gladys, Evelyn and Margaret were all born and brought up in. My grandfather was born in Branston, near the brewery town of Burton-on-Trent, but had somehow moved up north to work in the coal mines of Yorkshire. His wife, my grandmother Mabel, must have met Albert somehow, but before her marriage she had been Mabel White and her folks were an old Ryhill family.

Some of the happiest times of my childhood were spent in the living room of what was then the council house at 79 Mulberry Place in Ryhill. When the four Goodwin siblings gathered with other family members and talked about their upbringing in Ryhill, the laughs and the reminiscing ebbed and flowed.

My grandmother had been a cook in service to a rich mill owner in the nearby town of Dewsbury. This was before her marriage to my grandfather, who seemed to have endured a torrid time working down Brierley pit near Barnsley, where he sustained many injuries.

During the 1930s there was a little help for those with no money. Those not working for any reason were categorised as being 'on the parish'. Even though there was little or no money coming in, it seems as though every-one in my grandfather's house still ate well.

When the clan gathered, the stories between the siblings were batted back and forth – from tales of the perils of the outside toilets to the domesticated animal kingdom just across the wall at the back of Yardley Row, which back then was entirely dominated by allotments and livestock.

My dad was born in 1927. There was no welfare state then and no benefit system. This generation experienced means testing, where local officials used to barge in to people's houses and figure out if they had possessions of value that they could potentially sell to pay for themselves.

My dad told me that during the War he used to lay on his back on the roofs of the outside toilets, watching Luftwaffe bombers overhead, flying towards Sheffield in order to bomb the steelworks and the mines. As a wartime teenager, Dad used to chop sticks and do odd jobs and paper rounds, before helping out by carrying huge boxes of film for the projectionist at the Ryhill Empire Cinema, which used to stand on Chapel Street in Ryhill. He told me he got to see all the films free and his childhood crush was the actress Greer Garson. The site of the cinema is now occupied by two sets of semi-detached houses, right next to the village chapel. At the age of 14 my dad started work down Monckton colliery. The year was 1941.

*

Just like my dad before me I did odd jobs and a newspaper round. Dad was an underground rope splicer and weekend overtime was always available to him. He went underground just about every day of his life. I would be woken up by Dad and off we would both pedal on our bikes. We started together from our house and parted at the end of Station Road in Ryhill. Dad, who had by this time been transferred to Nostell Colliery, headed for the pit and I pedalled down to Bill Woodings' newsagents and bookmaker's shop.

Fridays and Sundays were the worst, as the already heavy newspaper bag was stuffed with local broadsheet papers the *Wakefield Express* and the *Barnsley Chronicle*. On Sunday, the newspaper sack was even more cumbersome, but it wasn't all hard work in all weathers. For a start, the faster I got on with my round the lighter the sack became. About halfway around my route there was a row of houses on Greenside, Ryhill. One of them had a sort of 'lean-to' porch, which was always left open and provided a temporary respite. In the cold, rainy or snowy weather, I used to enjoy being able to remove the sack from my shoulders for a few minutes and sit down on the carpeted floor listening for a few minutes as the weather did its worst and beat on the brattish cloth roof of my temporary shelter. I would listen to the wind and rain outside, whilst drying off and waiting for my second wind. Then I was off again, continuing past a pond, where geese belonging to the local midwife, Mrs Hopwood, used to chase me up the road towards the top of the village green. I then pedalled furiously down Briar Lane to finish my monster round.

My mum had trained as a concert pianist at the Royal College of Music and worked as my grandfather's pianist as a young girl. Her father, my grandfather, was Edward Margrave – a war hero who endured the hell of the trenches of Ypres in Belgium during World War One. Despite being wounded (through the neck) and gassed, he survived the Great War and went on to work as a professional singer, along with his stage singing partner Maurice Riding, in what was known as a tenor/baritone duet. Grandad was known professionally as Whistling Ted Marlowe and he was a fine tenor.

My grandmother had been born Anna Marie Tasker, and she told me as a child how proud she was 'walking out' with a soldier when my grandad was between battles and on leave. They married in 1915 and would remain wed for 61 years, until my grandma's death in 1976. My mum was the youngest of five. All her siblings were male and there was a 13-year age gap between her and the youngest of the four brothers Ralph. My older uncles were named Ernest, Arnold and Joe.

My mum qualified as a hairdresser and was also a theatre and club musician in her youth, but she followed none of her talents. Instead, while I was a small child, she worked in a succession of shop jobs in Wakefield and Barnsley. When Mum was 45 years old she became the oldest student nurse at college, and she qualified and stayed in nursing until her retirement.

As a result of my both parent's willingness to work and provide, my sister and myself went without nothing. Not even when my dad was on strike in 1971, when I was 12 and my sister was just about to start her training as a nurse – we still lived quite well.

All seems so normal. Then again, perhaps things always do seem normal to kids who are accustomed to their parent's version of what childcare actually means. My mum used to describe many of our neighbours as 'common' and I think she considered herself a cut above the people she had come to live amongst after her marriage to my dad in 1952.

As newly-weds my parents lived for a while with my mum's parents. My grandad had gone solo as a singer by then and also worked as club steward at Belle Vue Liberal Club in Wakefield, where he stayed until his own retirement. Many will remember the book written by Wakefield author David Storey, *This Sporting Life*. The film rights were acquired for the story that centred around a rugby player who played for Wakefield Trinity rugby league club. Grandad's club stood directly across the road from the Trinity stadium, where much of the action was filmed. The star of the film Richard Harris became a drinking buddy of my grandad's for the duration of the shooting.

*

4

UK schooling was going through changing and challenging times during my youth. At three years old I went to Ryhill and Havercroft Infants School, which was all about childcare, play, stories and an afternoon nap where when us tots snoozed around on gym playmats.

Then at the age of seven, we moved to Ryhill Junior School, on Chapel Street, where my dad and his sisters were schooled many years before in the same classrooms. I even own a picture of my dad where he looks about six years old, along with all his class mates, their little arms were folded behind their backs, as they posed for the camera in front of a huge wall map, which indicated that the British Empire at that time owned one third of the surface of the earth. Perhaps today such a map in a school would indicate what was of course closer to the truth, that our buccaneering wealthy ancestors travelled the world, competing with other colonialists by sticking the Union Jack willy-nilly into anything and everything they perceived to have any monetary value.

One day during a lesson by an avuncular Mr Chips-type teacher called Mr Hocking, who was indoctrinating us into Christianity by telling us all about scripture, I was asked to put down my pen, which was dipped in my inkwell at the time, and told to go home. While in the cloakroom I was asked by another teacher if I felt well. I admitted I had a severe headache. I looked aghast into the mirror and discovered I had a rash all over me. I was then asked to walk home, across farmer Henry Hammerton's cow fields where Mum was waiting. Before I was born my brother had died as a result of meningitis and there I was, at the age of seven, suffering from the same dreadful illness.

Our doctor was a GP called David Vining. Both he and the other GP, Hyman Shooman, operated out of a tiny little house complete with a small and chaotic waiting room, almost at the corner of Mill Lane and Cow Lane in Ryhill. At some stage in my dad's upbringing he must have been infected with the curse of racism and anti-semitism and he referred to our doctors collectively as the 'Jew-Boys' and their wives as 'Jewesses'. Doctor Vining was also the area National Coal Board emergency doctor, meaning that he was the doctor that went underground and attended the many serious underground accidents. I think my dad may possibly have blamed Doctor Vining for not diagnosing the meningitis that had killed my brother Steven. In any event they were the only doctor's in the area.

After many weeks of illness and a subsequent period of convalescence, I returned to school on the last day of term. There were two sweet shops on Chapel Street, Schofields and Turner's. Both of them had sent me presents while I was ill. I called in both shops en route to school to say thank you. I even saw my great auntie Beattie (known to one and all as 'Aunt Beat') who lived on Lafflands Lane, very close to the school and was afflicted with what is known as a cleft palate. I loved Aunt Beat and she had come to the school gates to welcome me back.

At the age of ten it was time to head for Felkirk Middle School, except that at that time it had only just become a middle school and only attained its new identity while I was there. The school-leaving age had just been raised from 14 to 16. This was the start of the great socialist educational experiment known as the Comprehensive Education System. My sister Barbara had attended the same school, when it was known as Felkirk Secondary Modern School. When she left there at the age of 14, she was enrolled at Barnsley Technical College, where she began a pre-nursing course.

I was at Felkirk until the age of 13. The school had a pet's centre and acres of grounds. It also had a tuck shop and a 'flat' in which older girls learned the finer points of cooking, cleaning and running a home. Perhaps providing this kind of facility to girls only would be frowned upon today.

I played for the school football team and passed into a coaching system organised by Huddersfield Town FC. The school boasted a huge veranda and the playtimes were epic in terms of the sheer numbers of kids out playing and engaging in games and sports. I just loved the place. I also boxed at the White Rose club in Wakefield after school.

I had an English teacher, William Foulds Leach, who was also a part-time actor with the stage name of William Wymar. While I was one of his pupils, he appeared in several episodes of *Coronation Street*. He played the part of a returning character who stayed in the soap for a few weeks back in 1971. The storyline involved Rovers Return landlady Annie Walker falling down a manhole and my teacher's character taking the blame for creating the danger which resulted in the accident. Mr Leach encouraged my love of writing, although his contribution to my school report admittedly stated that "stories are his forte, but Oh, how untidy he can be"!

But things were just about to change dramatically on the morning of my last day at Felkirk, as I chatted innocently to a man who had talked to me most mornings whilst delivering newspapers. Instead of waiting for the newspaper to be despatched through his letter box, this particular person waiting for me, along with a second man in his enclosed garden at the back of his house. The second man was holding a knife. Abuse comes in many forms and one thing I have learned is that those who choose to use children and young people for their own sexual gratification can be cunning and methodical. I was 12 years old and I now realise that what I experienced then shaped the way I reacted in all my future relationships.

*

5

I joined the class of '72 at a new school. I was shy, diffi-dent and quiet. I was quite bookish already, so perhaps teachers, parents and others did not spot the differences and the cracks in my personality and behaviour as they began to appear at my new school. I remember feeling insecure, self-conscious and so dirty. For a while I thought that hot baths may hold the answer to my feeling of being tainted. I used to bath in water which scalded me and as a result my skin was damaged. Certain smells that I remembered from the actual abuse incidents used to keep me awake at night. One teacher at school used the same smelly soap as was used by one of the abusers. I just couldn't go near him.

One day at school, during this poor teacher's History class, I asked to go to the toilet just to escape from the redolent smell of his soap. I was sought out when I did not return, but before then I had been outside in the school grounds for more than an hour vomiting and cry-ing. I was just 13 at the time and I told no one about my thoughts and feelings. My face, neck, shoulders and arms were covered in marks, where I had inexplicably burned or cut myself to shreds.

The new school I was attending was Willowgarth High School in the nearby village of Grimethorpe. The great socialist comprehensive system swung into gear and every day I would get on a school bus and head the four miles or so to the village, once famous for its colliery brass band and later as the setting for the hit film *Brassed Off*. The whole educational experiment was intense and was wonderful in theory but shambolic in practice. I was ambivalent and listless and had other things on my mind most of the time.

The area had become a mini-hub for the British film industry in 1970 as film-maker Ken Loach was in the area making the film *Kes*. Adapted from the Barry Hines novel *A Kestrel for a Knave*, one of the central characters was played by part-time actor and full-time coal miner called Freddie Fletcher. Freddie's brother David was a classmate of mine at high school.

The school at Grimethorpe had an original main block, but an east block, a south block and a music block had been added as well as a sports hall. The teachers were a gang of young socialists, appointed by an old socialist, the headmaster Mr Trotman, who had been a fighter pilot during the Battle of Britain.

Trotman wore the mortar board and used to swish around resplendent in his black cloak. Every day Trotman would arrive with a flourish of swift movement in the assembly hall. He would frequently regale us with stories of William Cowper and other early socialist writers of a different age.

The facilities at the school were new and pristine, but this was a rough, tough school. The kids all came from neighbouring villages and the bullying, fighting and general mayhem of so much youthful hubris, all thrown together, made it easy for someone like me, who just wanted to go through the motions and simply hide from reality.

At the age of 14, Maureen entered my life. She was 35 and her husband was in prison. I have never been able to look at women who resembled her since. Anne, the mother of a childhood friend of mine, also began her sexual interest in me around this time. Anne was divorced, and I provided the solution to her stated opinion that her bed was too big for one. Some people these days would describe the attention of these women to me as child abuse, but I told myself that I was just enjoying it all.

Many of us used to go 'potato picking' and 'pea pulling' at harvest times in farmer Mr Nobles' vegetable crop fields. Some local women joined in and they too expressed their sexual interest in some of the young lads present. These were the days when many more women were being prescribed with the contraceptive pill and some of them seemed keen to try out the its efficiency at every given opportunity.

The school-leaving age had been raised to 16 and in my three years at Willowgarth I achieved hardly anything at all. No one was checking up on the massive levels of absenteeism and truancy. Sometimes I would simply ride around the area on my bike. Frequently I would catch a bus to Wakefield and spend the day in the old Playhouse cinema on Westgate. On other occasions I headed for Barnsley Market, where I got to know a few traders and ended up doing odd jobs for them.

In my final year I would arrive at school and after making sure my name was ticked off in the register, I would duck out of school and head into Grimethorpe village where there was a pub called The Manor. There at just 15 or 16 I would play the miners at the then newly introduced game of 8-ball American pool. I made a lot of money out of this, until three burly and resentful blokes decided to end my time as a hustler by attacking and robbing me in the gents' toilet and that was the end of that.

What would happen when I left school? Well, it was hard to see any way forward, and at first I was on the dole and signing on every week at Royston unemployment office. Things had to get better and quick!

*

—6—

I started going into the local working men's clubs by fibbing about my age. The first club I was ever a member at was Ryhill WMC. This was the same club that my dad became a member at when he was 18. It was a rites of passage that sons followed their dads into club membership.

My lifelong love affair with live stage entertainment began at Ryhill and Havercroft social club, which was known locally as 'The Legion'. This club boasted a resident dance band and engaged visiting cabaret artistes. Amongst the first acts I saw was a singer and guitarist called David Van Dyke, and the Meers Brothers who played a bewildering multitude of musical instruments, as well as singing and being funny. Other favourites included singer and pianist Stan Richards, who later found fame as an actor in the rural soap opera *Emmerdale Farm* as Seth Armstrong. Ventriloquist Tony Addams and Granddad (his puppet) was also a great favourite.

I began to wonder how I might get involved in the then burgeoning club scene and place a tentative foot on the show business ladder. My mum just didn't think I could do it. Dad loved to sing, but Mum didn't particularly want to hear him and was dismissive of his attempts. We had a Steinway piano in our house, but Mum seldom wanted to play it.

Visits to the seaside on holidays always included taking

in a summer season variety show or two. Over the years I saw Jimmy Clitheroe in Great Yarmouth, Tommy Steele in Blackpool and 'Ten Ton Tessie' O'Shea in Torquay. The seeds were planted and I just had to find a way in.

In the meantime, I needed a job and I went along to Wakefield Trade Warehouse to be interviewed as a sales person and general factotum. The place was a DIY outlet, which stood on Cheapside in the middle of the city of Wakefield. The premises also included a kitchen and bathroom shop in one building and a bed store in another. The owners also ran a joinery in Sunderland Yard Wakefield, close to Kirkgate railway station and a storage facility in Smyth Street, adjacent to Westgate railway station. When I wasn't selling, restocking the shelves or unloading vans, I was also acting as an occasional delivery driver's mate. It wasn't much, but it was something.

*

My new employers were members of the Standring family and they were Jewish. This meant that I worked only half a day on Fridays and had Saturdays off. The time was made up by working until 8pm on Thursdays and from 9am until 2 pm on Sundays.

At the bottom of the garden of my parent's house at 79 Mulberry Place was a small field and a path which led to the cricket and football grounds. Nowadays the place is a full-on sports centre and social club. Back then it consisted of a children's park, a pavilion, tennis courts, a putting green and a magnificent bowling green. I had started crown green bowling at around the age of ten, but I never had the temperament to succeed at a game which requires high levels of patience, precision and concentration. I played every Saturday afternoon, but eventually gave it up at around 18 or 19 years old. Looking back, I think perhaps my interest in this sport was part of my lifelong obsession with doing jobs and hobbies which interest other types of people. Predictably perhaps, in the bowling team I was the only boy in a team consisting of middle-aged and elderly men.

Having not made it as a footballer, despite interest from Huddersfield Town FC and Barnsley FC, I started going to the match with a gentle quiet boy called Eddie Grainger. Eddie's uncle was Gordon Pallister, a former Barnsley player who ended up on the board of directors.

He gave Eddie two free tickets every matchday, and back then there was only one seated area at the Oakwell Stadium so we felt a little bit special by sitting in our posh seats in the West Stand.

Today Oakwell has three newish all-seater stands, but the original old wooden West Stand is still in operation. I still support the club and on matchdays I can be found in exactly the same seat I occupied as a child: West Stand Upper Tier Row L seat 32.

*

Weak-willed and easily led, but with lots of interests, I stumbled on towards my 18th birthday. My interests were judo, boxing, football, playing and performing music, crown green bowling and sex, but not necessarily in that order.

My mother and dad both wanted me to become a police officer. My mum because she was overbearing and determined that I should 'make something of myself'. My dad was also keen because I believe it was his ambition secretly as a younger man to become a bobby. Each and every night Dad would turn on a special radio he had somehow acquired and tune in to the police radio signal. The phonetic alphabet A for Alpha, B for Bravo C for Charlie etcetera was soon learned, but he was particularly interested in E for Echo, as this signal revealed live messages passed on by bobbies between each other patrolling our own village.

In 1977 at the age of 18 and a half, I was interviewed at the Bishopgarth police training school in Wakefield and to my astonishment I was accepted and began to train to become the top detectjve and law enforcer in the world (according to my mum at any rate). After a few week's induction at Bishopgarth, I was deemed ready to head for the former RAF Dishforth in North Yorkshire, which was then the area police training school.

The people doing the training fitted into two

categories. The majority were former military men, with medal ribbons on their chests, showing their service records. The other category was filled by younger smart-Alec types. The instructors were nightmarish, and a certain man-hating female sergeant was part of their team. She gave all the younger lads hell, whilst simultaneously accessing male and female sexual partners, all plucked from the masses of the young probationary bobbies.

In late 1977 a serial killer known by the grisly soubriquet of the Yorkshire Ripper was at large and it would be more than three years until the maniac, a Bradford lorry driver called Peter Sutcliffe, was finally collared. Along with other young probationary police constables, one afternoon in October 1977 I boarded a coach which headed to a police station in Leeds. My contribution to the capture of the Yorkshire Ripper was carrying huge boxes of files down some steps into a huge cavern of a room. I'm afraid this was the extent of my involvement in capturing the man who killed 13 women and attacked many others with a hammer before stabbing them repeatedly.

As was the case with my high school days, the facilities at RAF Dishforth were great but the staff were all there for a carefully orchestrated reason. To spot the most malleable and credulous junior bobbies and bully them into blind obedience. A documentary in the form of a television exposé later revealed the full extent of the problem.

At the time we ate rubbish and we were shorn like sheep during a time when longer hair was the norm. We slept in army-style dormitories and any movement around the site had to be conducted and orchestrated by marching in tight formation. One night, at the end of my time there, a big fight broke out in what was known as The Packhorse club, which was where the trainees and others went to socialise. I had simply intervened as peacemaker to try and break up the fight, as one of the lads involved was my 'next bunk neighbour'. A group of older male officers, along with another trainee – a nasty piece of work who, it transpired, was the brother of one of the instructors – all came wading in en masse. Self-righteousness, testosterone and alcohol are quite a combination, and the result quite predictably both bloody and lengthy.

The club was shut down on the spot, the obnoxious trainee went to hospital due to my pugilistic skills, but a combination of the sheer weight of numbers and tiredness resulting in me taking a lot of punishment. I didn't go to hospital, I went to bed and was awakened in the night, handcuffed and further beaten by the seven-strong gang, which included the aforementioned member of the training team, his brother and various other members of a gang resembling what I imagine the Hitler Youth looked like back in the 1930s.

The following morning was a bit of a blur. I just packed my things together and headed for the nearest railway station. I arrived in Wakefield and headed for Pinderfields hospital, where I had my broken jaw wired and received treatment for broken ribs and a fractured eye socket. A few days later a trip to the dentist's fixed some of my broken teeth and I rapidly came to the conclusion that my police career was well and truly over.

I never returned and I still have my resignation letter from the West Yorkshire police to this day.

*

—9—

Nursing my injuries, my mother seemed most concerned about the fact that all the neighbours and friends who knew about my new career may well have been chuckling away behind our backs at my failure to become a fully-fledged officer of the law. Mum badgered and cajoled me into looking around for another job as quickly as possible.

Various options were explored, but in the final analysis there was only one thing for it. Forget sport, forget music and get a job with my dad down Nostell colliery near Wakefield

In November 1977 I arrived at Allerton Bywater colliery near Castleford to begin underground training. I had been unemployed for just two weeks.

The city of Wakefield was a curious place back in the 1970s. While neighbouring conurbations like Dewsbury, Huddersfield and Leeds had all the mills and Barnsley and Rotherham were then filled with coal mines, Wakefield and towns within its postcode area, such as Pontefract and Castleford, had both.

The River Calder runs through Wakefield and observing the state of the river from the top of a bus travelling over the Chantry bridge back then was very revealing. The foam from the detergent emanating from the mills sometimes blew onto the road, such was its density. Nowadays the river runs clean, but back then, aside from pollution produced by the Wakefield mills, there was the slurry and waste from mine water and a multitude of other toxic waste including untreated sewage.

Nostell colliery had been opened and the original shafts sunk by the then Lord St Oswald of the Winn family in the early 19th century. Lord St Oswald still lived in the nearby Nostell Priory stately home when I worked at the pit. When his lordship expired unmarried and without children, the old lord's nephew became the new Lord St Oswald in 1980. He and his family still live there today. Coal mining had gone on in the area for hundreds of years and as a result Nostell colliery was a labyrinth of old shafts and tunnels going back to the days when monks from a nearby monastery used to mine the coal.

Before I went off to begin my underground training, I remember reflecting on how my poor old dad must have felt about his only son going down the pit. My grandfather had been a coal miner, as had his father Tristram. And now I was to spend far too long working in a variety of underground jobs, none of which I was much good at – and some of my experiences would shape my state of mind for life.

Visits to a great venue called Wakefield Theatre Club provided some light in the gloom and made me determined to become the next Martin Dale. Martin was the resident compere at this venue, which regularly hosted some of the biggest stars on the planet. Michael Jackson even appeared at the venue one evening, but the stars who stick out in my memory from that era included Tommy Cooper, Paul Daniels and the Nolan Sisters, who were the stars of the show on the evening of my 19th birthday.

I never became the next Martin Dale, or the next anybody for that matter. The variety clubs were going through their own death throes and eventually the Theatre Club became a fun pub, then a bowling alley, and has long been since demolished. I did become resident compere at a holiday park much later, but I had come along a bit too late for the big variety clubs which I had surely been born to work in.

For four weeks, along with other aspiring mine workers, we tramped around the Flockton seam training galleries at Allerton Bywater. We went through a coal face in another of the seams and on another training shift we helped salvage an old coal face unit, by rolling up lengths of conveyor belting, which was wet, sludgy and very heavy. Pit muck managed to reach everywhere on the human body. We chewed tobacco, in the belief that it kept the dust out of our respiratory systems. We deliberately overdosed on snuff at the end of the shift – the purpose was to make us sneeze so that the pit muck could be expelled out of our nostrils. In the pithead baths we rolled up the corner of the towels so we could get the dirt out of the corner of our eyes. To leave the dirt there would make us look as though we were wearing mascara. The pit muck seeped right into the pores of the skin and was all-invasive and all-consuming. There were no toilets down the pit and the shifts were seven and a quarter-hours in length with 20 minutes for 'snaptime' – our meal break.

*

—10—

It was January 1978 when I arrived with my dad for the first time at Nostell Colliery. It was 5.15am and there was a procedure to follow in the pithead baths.

Initially we had to walk past the time office and pick up our 'checks', which were counters with numbers on, enabling officials to see who was underground and who was not. We would go down to the side of the shaft and give one check to a man called the banksman, who kept them all in order. At the end of the shift we would then hand the other check in to the banksman to register that we had returned aboveground. My check number was 399.

Before all of that, we would troop into the 'clean side' of the baths and strip naked, leaving our clean day clothes and valuables safely in our lockers. We would then all walk through the actual shower area into the 'mucky side' to another locker where our pit clothes would be found. When I first started at the colliery, we had to provide our own pit clothes, but around 1979 we were provided with overalls etcetera, which would be placed in washbags and washed for us.

On that January morning I followed the crowd out of the baths, where we were provided with the opportunity of filling up our waterbottles. Then there was the option of a visit to the canteen, where some bought bits and pieces to take down the mine. After that we would walk up some stairs into the lamp room, where we would pick up a lamp, complete with a battery which would be attached to our belts. There was also a self-rescuer. This was a small and solid metal item which, like the bulky lamp battery, also attached to our belt. The purpose of the self-rescuer was that it would be attached to the nose and mouth in case of fire, thereby preventing death as a result of carbon monoxide poisoning. We wore boots with steel toe-caps and the whole get-up was completed by an electric flex, which went all the way up to our cap lamps, which clipped simply on to our safety helmets. The lamp itself contained two bulbs. The second, a weaker bulb, was simply there in case the larger one went out or became damaged. If both were smashed or damaged for any reason, the wearer would most probably have to feel their way out of the pit, as in most places underground there was no artificial lighting anywhere once away from the locomotive/underground transport roads. The darkness was inky black and all-enveloping.

After the lamp room we would walk over a sort of bridge/gantry area, before turning right and walking past the coal preparation plant (which pitmen referred to as the 'screens') where the coal ended up, once mined. This was our last chance to get our nicotine fix before our fag-ends would be discarded into the mud below. It was then a case of making our way through a series of air doors. At Nostell the main shaft was known as an upcast shaft, meaning air came up the shaft, after it had been circulated around the labyrinth of roadways within the pit.

The time had then come to board the 'cage'. At Nostell,

the cage in the No. 1 shaft had two decks. The bottom deck would be filled with men first, before the cage was lowered slightly by a man in a building called a winding house, which contained the winding gear many readers may be familiar with back in the days when pithead winding gear was visible to anyone passing by a colliery. The top deck would then be filled with men and down the pit we would plummet. Riders could disembark with the aid of a man called an onsetter, who would operate the cage once it had arrived at its destination, which was known as an inset.

There were four possible destinations on that cage at Nostell. After about 200 metres there was the by then worked-out Royston seam, which only remained open at that time as a second means of egress (emergency exit). About 150 metres deeper still into the earth there was the Yard seam and the Low seam, which were very close to each other. About half a mile into the earth was the Stanley Main seam, which was attached by roadway to the nearby Sharlston colliery, and the miners of Sharlston could also use this as an emergency exit themselves. At that point in the number one shaft there were duckboards, effectively closing off the remainder of the drop. Before they were placed there, there was also access into the very hot and sticky Kent seam, which was well over half a mile into the Earth. There was a much smaller number two shaft at Nostell. For ventilation purposes, the Kent seam was accessed by hundreds of very steep wooden steps, although on certain occasions the No. 2 shaft took riders right down to the Kent seam and over a demarcation line into the adjoining Sharlston Colliery.

Once onboard the cage and heading deep under-ground during my training at Allerton Bywater, I remember a strange feeling of acute anxiety coming over me. I think I put it down to nerves at the time. On the first morning at Nostell I had exactly the same feeling of foreboding as I disembarked from the cage to be met by a man called Jackie Daly, who checked my lamp and gave me a bit of a pep talk. The feeling of having the life squeezed out of me was enveloping me like an invisible tent. My head was bedecked with a yellow safety helmet, which was the sort of coal mining equivalent of a car driver's L-plate. I was introduced to another man called Jackie Turner, who I would be under the close personal supervision of for the next 20 days.

In the pit bottom, I remember looking across to a series of metal barriers, known as the pens, where men had to queue to get out of the pit at the end of the shift. I saw my dad standing there looking at me. If I had to describe his expression on that morning as he gazed over in my direction, I would have to say it was one of defeat and disappointment.

*

For the next four weeks, as a trainee, I was tagging along and being watched over by Jackie Turner. Jackie was a diminutive figure whose primary function down the pit was to look after the train tracks on the locomotive roads. He was also a member of the Communist party, but his grasp of politics seemed sketchy at best.

It was January and the underground roadways were ventilated via what was known as a surface drift. This was a huge roadway that went right to the surface from the bowels of the earth below and had a very steep gradient. The conveyor belt which carried all the coal and other materials went up the drift and found its way to the surface.

The next few weeks were bone-chillingly cold, as Jackie and I walked the tracks looking for problems, such as snecks in the line and fishplates (which joined rails together) which often worked loose. The only respite during the seven and a quarter hour shift could be found in the drift bottom cabin. This was basically a cavity in the wall in which pump water, which had warmed whilst pouring through the pipes from water pumps, produced a snug little nook in which to minimise the genuine risk of hypothermia.

The A638 road passes over a lake close to Nostell Priory stately home near Wakefield. Part of the pit roadway system went right under this lake, which meant that water from the dam seeped through to the mine workings, before being promptly pumped up to the surface again, 24 hours a day, seven days a week.

I was never taken into any active workings during this period, but I suppose my time with Jackie constituted a gentle, if freezing cold, introduction to life down Nostell colliery. I remember one morning during that period when I was provided with a pickaxe and instructed to walk up the drift and break off huge icicles which had developed due to the water seeping through and the cold winter weather.

By this stage in my life I had already met Melanie, who eventually in May 1982 became my first wife. I was an immature 22 year old and she was a mature 20 year old when we married. We had met in April 1977, when she was just 16 years old and I was 18. The marriage produced two children and ended in divorce after 21 years in circumstances I shall elude to later on.

*

Between January 1978 and January 1983, I was employed as an underground mineworker, performing a variety of roles. Once underground I used to experience nausea, a feeling of foreboding and what I now realise were actually panic attacks. All of which made me distracted, irritable and lacking concentration. Many years later it was revealed to me by a psychologist that, in her opinion, I was suffering acute claustrophobia.

Certain experiences underground over the next five years would also result in being diagnosed many years later with post-traumatic stress disorder.

The men I worked with during that time consisted of some of the best and worst people I have ever met in my life. Many of the men were great workmates and Nostell was known as a family pit, with many of the employees being related to each other. In fact, my mum's cousin Eric Margrave worked at the pit. A high proportion had been brought up in the rows of colliery houses in the nearby village of Crofton, which was known locally as 'Cribbins Lump'.

Instead of a long drawn-out story involving unintelligible mining jargon, I thought I would simply pick out a series of incidents which will hopefully retain my readers' interest and provide a glimpse of life as a Yorkshire coalminer.

It is also worth mentioning the fact that it was widely known at that time about my fledgling involvement on the

Clubland scene, where I had made friends. One pal was an entertainer called Antony McLochlan, who was born in the nearby village of Kinsley. Known by his stage name Tony Wayne, Tony was one of the first northern Clubland entertainers who were openly gay. A combination of inane stories, Chinese whispers and general mickey-taking, resulted in me being thought by some to be gay myself. This was despite the fact that I got married while I worked there and no one seemed to be able to produce or name anyone I had actually been 'gay' with.

I put up with what would be labelled homophobia these days, a bit weird I know since I am probably as heterosexual as it is possible to be, and for the most part I just laughed along. One day, one young man, who was probably none too secure about his own sexuality, overstepped the mark and my personal macho-bullshit meter went off the scale. I decided to make an example of him and the fight in the pit carpark was long and bloody. Aside from one lucky punch, which burst my lip and required stitches in my mouth, I inflicted considerable damage on my aggressor and soon he was off to hospital. I felt I had made my point.

In January 1978 I began to work as a timber lad/haulage worker in the Low seam. This seam was approximately 3foot 3inches thick so that was the space that face workers operated in for long periods. The job on the haulage entailed groups of us taking materials on a rope haulage system right up to the coal face line. The materials consisted of bits of timber, which were all used for many and various functions on the coal face. The biggest items were 'rings', which were the metal girders which helped hold up the roof. This particular unit (section of coal) was coming to the end of its life and within a few weeks I was moved to perform the same job on the next unit to be mined in the Low seam.

At that time, I was involved in a few fist fights and other such shenanigans. To some I was an outsider and it showed. An ex-police officer who mixed with gay people made me quite a target. Foolish people usually believe what they want to believe when it comes to unpopular men. I was young, fearless, martial arts trained to black belt standard, and I just didn't care whether people liked me or not.

There were two forms of coal mining: advance and retreat. On advance, the coal face was moved forward as two tunnels running parallel to each other and known as the loader gate and the tail gate advanced, and therefore the tunnels gradually became longer. The air underground only travels one way and a series of airtight doors determines the direction of the airflow. In the tail gate, explosives would be used by a man called a shotfirer. The rock above the coal had to be removed. This was known as rock ripping, and once this was blown to pieces it was packed into the walls by hard-working men who were known as rippers. When we were in the tail gate, after the shotfirer had done his thing, the smoke of what was known as 'powder wreak' combined with general pit dust was all quite visible as it approached us, in the shape of a dense shroud of fog. We would sit still, wearing dust masks, until the wreak had cleared. Once the noxious cloud had passed by within the airflow, work resumed and another shear of coal could be cut by a huge metal pick-armed piece of machinery called a shearer.

Not too long after moving on to the new unit, we were tasked with removing huge pieces of rock ripping which had fallen off a new and very short and wobbly conveyor belt. A huge shard of this material fell off the belt just I was grappling to remove another large piece and my left hand was squashed, with every bone in the hand broken. I was taken to hospital, my hand was vigorously scrubbed, while a couple of bones were actually sticking through the flesh. Surgery followed and my left hand was encased into a plaster cast for six weeks.

Returning to work in late 1978, I had very limited and somewhat impaired grip in my left hand and was attending hospital appointments for physiotherapy. As a result, I was deployed temporarily as a 'button man'.

A series of conveyor belts took the coal through the mine roadways and off towards the surface. At various intervals the roadway would change direction and a new section of belt would begin. That meant that at each of those points in the chain of conveyors, a man would have to be deployed to stop and start the belt and keep the area tidy and safe.

We 'button men' were completely alone in the darkness with no one present for hundreds of metres in either direction. I never told a soul about the constant panic I felt whilst quite alone. Being a voracious reader (even to this day) I used to devour lots of books, which I slipped into a bag and read underground by the light of my cap lamp bulb. The job was pretty much a watching brief, with a bit of cleaning and shovelling here and there. It was classed as light duties, due to the state of my left hand.

In 1979 I was moved into the Yard seam and still on light work duties, I was on another button, which was very close to the freezing cold railway locomotive roads I had tramped up and down with Jackie Turner. Jackie's son Brian worked on the next button down and he and I became great friends. I remain in touch with Brian courtesy of the magic of Facebook to this day.

A little later I started work back on the haulage and trained for the coal face on another newly opened unit. While working in that area, we were informed that a hot-shot reporter from the *Daily Mirror* was visiting to write a report, which was subsequently headlined, 'Down Below with the Top People'. I still have the newspaper clipping and the aforementioned hotshot's name was Bel Mooney. Bel and I are friends to this day and she now works as a sort of agony aunt for the *Mail on Sunday*.

Along with a group of workmates, we had our photos taken for the *Daily Mirror* on the surface at the end of the shift. Bel stayed with us and described her time underground as 'A Living Picture of Hell'. Years later she told me that her biggest concern was that there were no toilets underground and when she asked about nipping off for a pee, she was told to walk off down the tail gate and squat down. Bel declined this suggestion, but told me years later she was really crossing her legs after seven and a quarter hours underground.

*

It was at this juncture that I was invited to join the safety team, and during this period there were three fatal accidents. The men who died down Nostell Colliery during my time there were Alan Palfreyman, Dennis Brook and Paul Thomas. Out of respect for these three gentlemen I won't go into the details of how they all were killed. Instead I will just say that the three were killed underground in a series of entirely separate and tragic incidents. I helped deal with the aftermath of two of these deaths. The mental images I still visualise haunt me still.

And then during my work, one day in 1982 I was rendered unconscious in an incident where myself and two other men were overcome with noxious gases. On another memorable morning I was quite alone riding on the cage (the structure which transported men up and down the pit shaft). The structure hit the side of the shaft and I was bounced around like a conker on a string. A man called Kenny Bryan, who was a good friend, had the job of trying to secure the cage to the spot where men were meant to step off. The drop below me was a good quarter of a mile and if the rope mechanism broke, that would have been the end of my life. I remember screaming, "Get me off! Get me off!" Eventually I managed to step off the cage to safety. I must have looked like a gibbering wreck. Oddly enough my dad was standing in the pit bottom area at the time and he never turned a hair.

I often wonder what was going through his head at the time.

During the same period of my terror on the cage, I remember walking into a heading, which was a roadway under construction and in which there was only one way in and one way out like a sort of underground cul-de-sac.

People imagine that roof falls underground manifest themselves with falls of rock from the roof – and they did sometimes. What might surprise many is that 'side-weight' is more common, in which the side of the road-way reveals its pressure when small slivers of strata drip off the walls. Another sign of a mine roadway under pressure is 'floor-blow', which produces huge lumps in the floor of the tunnel to come upwards. Maintenance men come along and dig out the floor periodically in order to preserve the integrity of the tunnel.

On one memorable morning, I was doing a job in a heading for the ventilation officer Tony Morrison. The 'weight' suddenly came on and, along with the other eight men in the heading tunnel, we ran for our lives to escape being buried in the collapse. The workings were abandoned but everyone made it out of the tunnel – just!

On the subject of Tony Morrison, I behaved disgracefully to him on more than one occasion and I look back on that with deep regret. I heard years later that Tony had become embroiled in a murder enquiry, when his wife Bridget was diagnosed as terminally ill. She was suffocated in a mercy killing by Tony. Years later I was in a pub in Wakefield talking over a business deal, when I spotted

Tony and also noticed that he was eavesdropping my conversation. I regret to say I pretended not to notice him. To this day I wish I had spoken to him and apologised.

On another occasion I was inspecting a roadway for what was known as second means of egress, a sort of emergency exit in the event of roof falls. A huge and very smelly pool of water had gathered in a dip in the tunnel. Afterwards, in the pit showers I could not stop scratching my legs, and the lower part of my body.

By then, after much acrimony on the home front, I had moved into a bedsit in Wakefield, where I woke up that day from my afternoon post-shift siesta and found I could not open my eyes, due to huge swellings around my eyelids. The itching all over my body was intense and unrelenting and I felt quite grim. I took a taxi up to the casualty A&E department at Pinderfields Hospital in Wakefield. I had to be helped into the place by a kind stranger, who of course I couldn't actually see. I was admitted to hospital and while the precise nature of some of the weal marks on my body were never really diagnosed, subsequent blood tests revealed that I had contracted Weil's Disease (also known as Leptospirosis) which is most often transmitted by rat urine.

Coincidentally, exactly six years to the day that I first ventured underground at Nostell, in January 1983 the lower part of my body was crushed, after slipping under a heavy piece of machinery in wet conditions. I was placed on a stretcher and given morphine (there were secure and sterile morphia safes underground). While on the stretcher I was very nearly run over by a small loco-motive, which the driver seemed to lose control of.

I sustained serious leg, knee, foot and ankle injuries, as well as wounding to my hip area. For the next eight months I underwent three operations and somehow managed to keep my lower leg. A claim for negligence was lodged by the National Union of Mineworkers on my behalf, and when I returned to work the following September, I was deployed on light duties on the surface, where I made a great friend in a young man called Geoff Neville. At that point I had decided that the life of a mineworker was not for me and my intention was to wait until my negligence claim compensation was paid out and then leave. The main snag was while I was waiting for the claim to be settled, the biggest and longest indus-trial dispute in history began.

This was open warfare with the prime minister Mar-garet Thatcher describing we miners as 'the enemy within'. The strike lasted for a year and technically I was still on the books throughout the whole class struggle in which we fought for jobs and our communities.

All the time I worked at the pit I also operated on the club live band scene and was always being told I should go solo as a singer. I also operated an agency and, after a mention of my new business in *The Stage and TV Today* newspaper (as it was known then), the postman arrived with a full sack of advertising material sent by performers from all over the UK. Known as Footlights Agency for a time, I was the youngest licenced entertainment agent in Great Britain. My licence number was YH788.

In short, I was a terrible agent and the learning curve was huge. I operated the agency business from a small terraced house that myself and my wife at the time bought for £8,500 in my home village of Ryhill. The house at 63 Station Road was said to be haunted. So, there I was, living in a haunted house, running an entertainment agency very badly and accepting my first solo singing engagements. In between all of that I was doing my bit on the picket lines and trying to run a club which I had been elected on to the management committee of, which stood just a few doors from my home. Back then it was known as Ryhill Working Men's Club.

With so much going on, what could possibly go wrong?

*

—14—

During the miners' strike of 1984 and 85, the oppressive atmosphere in the pit villages hung over everyone like a cloud. The local parish hall became a centre where mining families could obtain groceries. The TUC set up the campaign 'They Shall Not Starve'. The communities pulled together as the press and wider media launched their smear campaign.

A man called Roger Windsor had been planted by the secret service MI5 into a job in the accounting department at the National Union of Mineworkers headquarters in Barnsley. The right-wing press published that the miners' union president Arthur Scargill was taking money from the Libyan dictator Colonel Gaddafi, which even a village idiot would have found hard to believe, but to *Sun* readers it would of course sound perfectly reasonable.

Shadowy figures, often protected by uniformed policemen with no numbers on their epaulettes, wandered around the pit villages in search of traitors and the weak and most vulnerable. It was later discovered these were not policemen at all. They were believed to be hired heavies and military people, as were many of the lorry drivers who were hired to drive through the picket lines

My wife Melanie was involved politically, as was I myself for that matter. I was a local Labour Party official and she was on the National Executive Committee at the

Banking Insurance and Finance Union. In the midst of the strike, we were both invited to many political gatherings and the atmosphere was supercharged with mystery, intrigue and violence.

The strike was completely solid in Yorkshire, but in Nottinghamshire a so-called 'scab union' funded by Thatcher's government, was set up – the Union of Democratic Mineworkers formed by a man called Neil Greatrex. This slippery character was convicted after the strike for the cooking the books and 'trousering' much of the scab union's cash.

Peter McNestry was head of a staff association called NACODS – the National Association of Colliery Overmen Deputies and Shotfirers – which became pivotal to the whole dispute. Their members, with their jobs on the line too, voted overwhelming to support the NUM in the strike. Despite the vote McNestry did a deal with the destructive American strike-breaker Ian MacGregor, who Thatcher had brought in especially for the job in hand. In the ultimate act of treachery, irony and betrayal, McNestry was later put in charge of something called the Coalfields Regeneration Plan, which was designed to try and rebuild the communities destroyed by Margaret Thatcher – the very jobs and communities his decisions whilst running NACODS had helped cause the permanent loss of.

A few days before the end of the sulphurous year-long strike, I attended a mass meeting of Yorkshire miners which was held at Castleford Civic Centre. Arthur Scargill addressed a gathering packed in like sardines and, barring much of the press and a few secret service people no doubt, every one of us present was dedicated to not capitulating to the Tories. The following morning *The Sun* newspaper reported that Scargill had addressed "the last handful of bedraggled and defeated striking miners and their families".

As in any war, the women in the mining villages became a real driving force. I shudder to think what would have happened if any of these tough and determined women had ever got within punching distance of Thatcher.

A scab was the name for a strike-breaker. "Once a scab-always a scab" was the mantra but eventually the cracks began to show. In Nottinghamshire and the Midlands many of the miners were scabs and worked throughout the entire strike.

I remember ringing the Nostell Colliery union secretary Norman Hartshorne one day, towards the end of the strike in 1985. Norman was a great man who later became the mayor of Wakefield. He appears again later on in my story. I had rung Norman up about my compensation claim, which had been suspended. The strike had been declared illegal and the government had sequestrated the union's funds. In the eyes of the striking miners 'sequestrated' was just another word for 'stolen'. I could hear the emotion in Norman's voice when he informed me, "We've got some scabs in."

The trickle of scabs became a flood and the strike was lost after exactly one year. Although technically no longer an underground worker, I was still on the books and I proudly joined my old workmates and marched back to work behind the colliery banner with the brass band playing.

Under two years later Nostell colliery along with hundreds of others was closed and lost forever. The UK still imports coal, largely for the by-products and chemicals which are produced from it. Some of the coal comes from countries who, for a start, must think we are crazy for importing from them, as the British Isles still has hundreds of years of untapped coal reserves, while some of the coal comes from places in the world where they still send small children underground to do their dirty and dangerous work.

Hundreds of pits and thousands of communities were lost back then and there are no working coal mines in the UK today, despite Thatcher's ad nauseum proclamations promising that "there was no pit closure programme in existence".

*

I have already mentioned helping to run the working men's club in Ryhill. I was show-business mad, but sadly this club was hardly Caesar's Palace. Just after I jumped onboard the management committee as concert secretary, Prince Charles was about to marry the then Lady Diana Spencer. The whole country seemed to be out partying on the big day and we had booked a band to entertain in the club.

The evening went well, until a local gang led by a thoroughly poisonous lad called Stevens decided to cause problems. There was a huge fight during which, along with others, I got stuck into this gang physically. Stevens seemed able to exert a considerable negative influence on his numbskull mates, who even referred to themselves as his 'gang'. He was seldom around however once the trouble he had instigated actually broke out. I was pretty fearless back then and I walked away after the fight, emerging bloodied but unbowed, even though I was well outnumbered. Other fights were going simultaneously at the time and the whole street was filled with violence and mayhem.

A gentle lad called Rob McGraw, who was simply trying to get away from the area quickly, was savagely set upon by members of the Stevens gang and his head hit a kerbstone. Rob was badly beaten up and everyone thought he was dead at the scene. A trip to hospital revealed horrendous head injuries and Rob subsequently lost most of his faculties. The last I heard of this splendid young man, he was permanently confined to a wheelchair and was physically and mentally disabled. Two members of the gang, whose names are not important enough to mention here, went to prison, unfortunately not for anywhere near long enough sentences.

My daughter Michelle was born while my house close to the club was for sale. A lady bought it for £13,500 and we didn't mention the odd atmosphere of the dwelling and the local stories of the house being haunted. The ghosts were said to be those of a mother and son, who used to run the place as a shop where once crockery and hardware was sold. We moved out of the village and, complete with new baby, we moved into a brand-new house in the village of Altofts near Castleford. Leaving Ryhill felt like a weight was being lifted off me.

When the Covid-19 lockdown was going on, we reached a phase of 'travel around a bit' ambiguous advice, so I took a drive back to Ryhill one afternoon. I walked with my two Old English sheepdogs Stan and Ollie, down an old railway track that used to be home to the Ryhill and Wintersett railway station and we headed towards the Wintersett Reservoir. Its 'woodland meets water' location reminds some travellers of the Catskill Mountains in America.

Along with my boy-hounds I traversed a circle, which began at the old station, where I had headed off on a family holiday to Great Yarmouth in 1966 on a steam train. My canine companions and I soon reached a point where an old railway bridge used to be. There is a field which leads back into Ryhill which we used to call the 'Dockshire'. The pathway still exists and I became aware of a jogger headed in the same direction and coming up behind us. Dogs are such a boon when it comes to meeting and making contact with people. I soon discovered this lady had only recently moved into Ryhill and had lived and worked previously in Bangladesh.

My new friend, attracted no doubt initially by Stan and Ollie, was soon asking me about the Ryhill of the past and bemoaned the fact that there are no pubs in the entire village these days. I told her all about the pubs that used to be there and about the village I grew up in. Ryhill is now firmly part of the Leeds commuter belt and my new friend was surprised to discover that the Ryhill I was born in back in the late 1950s was once a dormitory mining village.

After we parted, I headed back to my car, which was parked near where the old railway station used to be. I walked down Station Road, past the club, which is still running as one of the so-called Sam Smith's brewery venues – and these days the place does not feature music of any kind. In fact, as I gazed through the old foyer door, there was a noticeboard with a sign emblazoned with colourful ink which barred swearing and the use of mobile phones on club premises.

The club has become exactly what we were trying to

get away from in 1980. Perhaps there is a lesson to be learned there in the fact that Ryhill village club still exists at all these days, albeit merely as a place to meet, chat and have a beer.

*

—16—

When we arrived with our new baby daughter at 58 Rose Farm Approach, Altofts, and moved in, the estate was still a building site. But the house was smart and modern and I was accepting solo gigs. I knew I would need a stage name if I was the join the actors' and entertainers' trade union Equity. My real surname is Goodwin. I honestly can't remember why, but we ended up deciding on 'Mark Ritchie'.

At first it was all about picking up gigs here and there, which was a successful strategy. Learning on the job was what it was all about and I found I could work every night if I wanted to. At first the Mark Ritchie gigs consisted of singing in pubs and smaller social clubs. Accompanied by backing tapes at first. I soon discovered that owning written musical arrangements for the clubland resident musicians was a prerequisite for any singer trying to move forward at that time. I also learned that if I could find the right agent, I could access bigger and better work.

My first weekend as a solo singer began at Rotherham Borough Transport club, where I discovered that being onstage alone was very different to working in a live band. I made the mistake of taking a drink onto the stage with me. I was so nervous that my trembling led to spillage. It was then on to Kinsley Greyhound Stadium near Pontefract for a Saturday night gig, before finishing the weekend at Jacksonbridge club in Huddersfield. And there it was, my career as a solo full-time professional entertainer was up and running.

*

—17—

Off I went, straight into the world of the professional entertainer and working regularly, mainly in the then still fairly vibrant social club scene.

Henry Solly was a 19th-century philanthropist and religious educator, who expressed a desire to improve the education of working men. He came up with the original idea of the working men's club. Astonishingly some clubs are still known as WMCs to this day, although most have changed or adjusted their names to become more gender neutral. As amazing as it may seem, some clubs had men-only rules and their antiquated approach to business was in so many cases jaundiced by self-interest. Most clubs were run by management committees, invariably made up of men who were employed in industry etcetera during the day, but at night become part-time music and entertainment promotors.

In 1974 there were over 4,500 clubs within the Club & Institute Union operating in the UK. The C&IU exists as an umbrella organisation, representing the interests of most social clubs and remains in operation to this day. Nowadays the number of clubs in the UK has more than halved since the 70s heydays. The clubs seem largely irrelevant to the leisure needs of the young these days. Some are trying to reinvent themselves as family-friendly community centres.

For the last 35 years I have been entertaining in clubs

with ageing memberships. With haemorrhaging visitor numbers year after year I have been operating in a business environment where the club businesses have attempted to survive in an area of the leisure market which has been openly discriminating against roughly half its target audience: women.

In some clubs, even today, women are not allowed to become full club members, and although most eventually woke up and smelled the business coffee in recent times, most have effectively excluded an entire generation of prospective customers.

Nonetheless there was still a living to be made back in the 80s as an entertainer in the clubs, even though the ladder to success were already being removed. Back then the rungs of the ladder began in the pubs and then up to regular club work. The higher you climbed the more chance you had of being booked into the big variety clubs, which still existed. You then had a chance to land a spot in a summer season show at a seaside theatre. From there the entertainer may well have been spotted and invited to appear as a guest on a telly variety show. Nowadays you are either a live entertainment professional in the clubs, holiday parks and on the cruise ships, or you are nothing.

The incontrovertible truth is that the university graduates began to run telly during the 80s and their undergrad humour dictated that going to the right university would allow you to meet the right people for those who wanted to be famous and on the telly.

The only alternative is the 15 minutes of fame on offer

from the Simon Cowell talent show circus, and the least said about all that the better! Although, towards the end of my story, I will pick up on the knotty subject of Mr Cowell and his cohorts and my involvement with them later on.

*

18

Instead of trawling through my diary and work records from my years as a professional entertainer in the clubs, holiday centres and general show business jobs, I will simply flag up the rare highs and the depressingly frequent lows from down the years.

The highs were few, and whenever I did stumble into any decent work, I almost invariably made a complete dog's breakfast of things and the opportunities were all lost. The reason can only be my temperament and the state of my mental health, but more about all that later.

Those in the know when I became a professional entertainer told me that it took at least 18 months to become established as a Clubland entertainer, no matter how talented you were. I found work fairly easy to come by, although it was often very poorly paid.

In 2020 I believe I have come full circle and then even further down. Nowadays I find work very difficult to come by, and in comparative terms I am still very poorly paid.

Entertainment agents are a singularly odd breed of businesspeople. The legal relationship between agents and entertainers is that the entertainer technically employs the agent and the agent chooses whether or not to represent the entertainer. Then, as now, many agents don't see it that way and perceive themselves as The Boss within this most tenuous of relationships.

Since the very beginning of my solo career I have kept a diary. This was not merely for keeping records for my accountant and the tax gatherers. I also devised a code which told me approximately how full the room was where I was working, and how well I felt when I was working on any given night. I also marked the audience as any one of the following:

'Excellent'
'Very Good'
'Good'
'Fair'
'Poor'
or 'Not Worthy of Mention'.

In the clubs there was always an obsession with the great game of bingo. As Clubland entertainers we were all resigned to the fact that, no matter how good a night we were having in a working men's club, we were always playing second fiddle to the bingo.

The clubs used to book the acts independently back in the old days by simply ringing them up on the phone. By the early 70s the agents were exerting their control over all the bookings at most clubs. Agent cliques formed and agents who were chums with fellow agents swapped their roster of 'managed acts', effectively operating a business cartel by keeping the acts represented by the agents they were not friendly with out of certain clubs. This warped and unfair system exists to this day in what remains of the once great and proud club movement.

It became clear to me very quickly that I needed to cultivate the acquaintance of some agents and fast!

*

19

My diary records from those early days indicate that agents who supplied me with work at the very beginning were a pretty chequered band of small-timers.

There was a club organist called John Hardcastle. Judith Walker was an agent I did a lot of business with who was playing at the agency business whilst trying to hold down a full-time job. I hold very fond memories of an agent called Michael David, who used to send me to Dewsbury Moor club on a Tuesday evening for the princely sum of £18 and then take 15 per cent off that as his commission. All Michael's other work offered similar rewards – all bargain basement clubs and all of which have since disappeared off the Clubland map, such as Hall Road club in Leeds, Laughton Common club near Rotherham and Dewsbury socialist club.

Michael was a singer and drummer. His roster of acts consisted of Dene Michael, a singer who would later go on and find fame as part of the infamous party band Black Lace who introduced the world to 'Agadoo', and Shelley Stevens, a singer who later emigrated to Australia and who I visited back in 2009. The rest of the acts on Michael's books all contained him in the line-up. JJ Jones was Michael singing solo under a stage name. Revive 45 was Michael in a duo with a mate who was a guitarist. Penthouse Suite was Michael with his mate on guitar and another mate on bass guitar, and Unit Four Plus Two was

Michael with some entirely different musicians who he had enjoyed some chart success with, due to a one-hit wonder titled 'Concrete and Clay'.

Becoming established was the key, and during those early years the work was hardly lucrative but it constituted a paid apprenticeship. In 1986 I worked 264 nights out of 365, and some venues became regular haunts.

Brudenell social club in Leeds held a citizen band radio users' social evening every Thursday. My songs formed part of an evening where a bunch of rather sad types compared CB radios, with the occasional muttering of "Rubber Duck", "break-a-break" and "ten-ten till I hear you again" clearly audible. Whilst not onstage, I used to hide in the dressing room trying in vain to stifle my chuckling.

The Entertainer was a club in Dewsbury where I would arrive quite late in the evening to entertain at the 'grab-a-granny night'. Middle-aged ladies, many apparently desperate for sex, would ogle me, believe it or not. Many wanted to take me home with them. Viagra wasn't invented back then, but even if it was there would not have been enough supply of the stuff in the world to induce me to succumb to the charms of these mature Yorkshire belles.

Pete Sadler was an agent who worked out of his office in Chesterfield. His instructions to artistes he booked when working the chain of mainly North Derbyshire clubs that he supplied, was to sing only 50s, 60s and rock'n'roll songs. This, as I soon found out, was mainly due to the fact that Pete himself only listened to 50s, 60s and rock'n'roll.

Benny Britton was an agent from Sheffield who used to boast that the commission I paid him would ensure his house always had fitted carpets. I never really understood that.

Toby Major spoke with a very thick Eastern European accent and his answering machine messages and general conversations were virtually unintelligible. Walking into Toby's office in Leeds one day, I noted his premises were right next to a small cemetery. "This is where we bury all the Clubland comedians after they die on their arses onstage," he casually informed me.

Jim Andrews was a large man who ran an agency with his wife Ellen. Jim had a florid face and loved to give advice. It was Jim who upped my fee to £60 for a weekend booking.

Bill Turner ran AMA, also known as The Artiste Management and Agency, in Doncaster. Bill was a smooth operator in the clubs. I was sorry to hear that he hadn't made old bones, due to the dreaded Alzheimer's disease, which was later to claim his life.

I learned a great deal from the agent Owen Hammond, who was in the twilight of his career but had once been very big. Steve Middleton ran Metro Management and his skills as an agent were never fully exploited due to his premature and tragic death on the operating table.

Johnny Winstanley used to supply all the live backing musicians to the clubs until gradually the use of backing tracks, in those days on tape, drove the affable Johnny out of business.

Steve Jackson had been part of an act called The Merry

Macs, with his wife and the aforementioned actor and pianist Stan Richards. His agency office in Barnsley overlooked the Oakwell football stadium and I used to chat to him at the match about this and that. Steve gave me a lot of work. He died in 2019.

Geoff Barber was a Pennines farmer who also ran an agency. Geoff was a nice man who died way too young.

Chris Gordon was too sly for his own good! Financial irregularities earned him the nickname 'Robber Gordon' and one could always tell when he was lying as his lips were moving.

George Green was a South Yorkshire agent who loved a drink, probably too much. But he was nice to me and was coming towards the end of his career and his life by the mid-80s.

The first time I ever worked solo at a holiday park was in the genteel Yorkshire resort of Filey on June 8th 1986. Dennis's South Shore Holiday Camp was the name of the venue and I honestly have no recollection of the gig whatsoever, so I must have been distinctly 'underwhelming' to the happy holiday audience. Over the ensuing years, holiday parks were to provide a hugely substantial part of my income as an entertainer.

In the July of 1986 I was booked to open a new venue near Fleetwood on the Fylde coast of Lancashire. It was a late-night job and the owners offered me a caravan to kip in overnight. The mother of all summer thunderstorms hit as I slept and it seems the caravan was struck by lightning. I woke in the middle of a blinding flash, with the rain beating down on the caravan roof and it seemed the caravan actually arose and then fell with a crash. I packed up quickly, got in the car and drove home through the storm. My rationale was that, if I was going to be killed by lightning, I would rather make it a little more difficult for the god Thor by at least presenting him with a moving target.

John Bridges ran the Dukeries agency and I started receiving a few gigs from him at about this time. One Saturday was quite lucrative, with an early evening gig at Hendon Rise social club in Nottingham, before I moved on to a late-night drinking club in the same city named the High Society bar.

Claude Hunter was an agent who was openly gay and worked from an office within a miner's welfare club. Claude was brave and honest, but during the panic caused by emergence of the Aids epidemic, Claude was on the receiving end of much homophobia. This abrasive character had a caustic line in wit and, due to his bad feet, often came out into the clubs wearing smart suits on his back and comfy slippers on his poor feet.

A regular Monday evening double-booking saw me performing an early spot at the Arundel club in Sheffield, before travelling to nearby Rotherham for a spot at the Trades club later on. The first time I took these gigs saw me working with a great comic and singer called Simon Ashley. The Trades closed only recently, while the Arundel, a club which was so large and scary to some entertainers, was a venue I continued to work at on and off through the ensuing years.

Holmewood social club in Bradford was notorious. No

car in living memory had survived on their carpark for more than one hour before being either damaged or broken into. I foolishly left some equipment in the back of my van there one night and the van window was smashed and the equipment stolen. The idiots who stole all of this tried to sell it on to a musical instruments shop in Bradford, where the owner and I knew each other. The police were called, the lads were nicked and eventually I recovered my equipment.

Agents can be quite elusive and even secretive about their day-to-day work. An agent from the West Yorkshire town of Brighouse called Jeff Wilson has been giving me work for over 35 years on and off, and I'm still yet to meet him.

On September 5th 1986 I was booked on to a variety show at Wakefield Theatre Royal and Opera House. The celebrated Victorian theatre architect Frank Matcham built this delightful chocolate-boxy theatre in my own home town and I was delighted to be on the show. I was even interviewed about the cast and show on BBC Radio Leeds. On the night, aside from a great band called Rocking Express, the rest of the cast seemed to be made up of members of the am-dram brigade and the show went down like a knackered lift. After this disastrously poor evening, I walked across the stage and took in the atmosphere in the by-then empty house. I told myself I would be back there one day and I would do myself justice the next time around. I have never been on that stage since. Who knows, perhaps there is still time for me?

Belle Vue WMC in Wakefield was a tiny little venue.

When I worked there for the first time, my main memory was of an odd green cubicle, which was perched incongruously on the tiny stage. No bigger than a toilet unit, I was amazed to be told that this was in fact my 'dressing room'.

The Portobello hotel in Wakefield used to book me regularly for their monthly tenants and residents' association functions. The gig appeared in my diary and I arrived to find a large group of Gypsies/Travellers from a nearby camp. Barred from everywhere, the group had somehow convinced someone to let them in and mayhem ensued. After a mass brawl broke out, during which my main consideration was to protect my expensive PA system and amplifier, the floor of the concert room was covered in pools of blood and even a bitten-off human ear. Some of the protagonists eschewed the option of heading to hospital to get stitched up. I was therefore asked to perform another set of songs to people who were slipping around in blood as they danced. I managed to escape unscathed with my equipment undamaged, and for that I was extremely grateful.

The Carriage and Waggon welfare club in Derby was a great venue and on the night of my appearance the comedian and impressionist Les Dennis had been invited to the club to present a charity cheque, while I provided the entertainment. Years later I was involved, albeit slightly, in a TV show that Les was featured in. I reminded him of that evening, but the whole thing seemed to have slipped his mind. Odd really, as the name of the club where we first met is pretty hard to forget!

I was still actively involved in the Labour Party at that time and I agreed to appear at a fund-raising event in a club. Some people who knew me came along mainly to take the mickey and I didn't take their derision well. As ever I stewed on my anger for quite a while before violence ensued at a later date. Even back then I should have been considering the possibility of my mental health being impaired. But there was such a stigma back then that I kept things bottled up, before lashing out suddenly and unexpectedly. Up until my late 50s, this remained unchanged and I have been so lucky that I have never been convicted of any acts of violence and have never been sectioned into psychiatric care.

In October 1986 I took a booking at Hexthorpe club in Doncaster. This night stands out in my memory as in real terms I was sexually assaulted by a group of very drunk females. As I left the club later, I saw the leader of this gang of harridan females going back to what I assumed to be her home. This was very close to the place where comedy stars Ronnie Barker and David Jason had filmed the sit-com *Open All Hours*. The shop in the programme was not a grocer's shop at all. It was in fact a hairdressing salon. I drove home considering my future employment options very carefully.

The so-called 'fun pubs' still operated back then. Owned mainly by gay business people, venues such as the Santa Fe Bar in Halifax were truly great fun. I worked there one night with a comedian called Arnold Clockworthy. This was basically a young man who took hours of make-up to appear as a very old man. 'Arnold' was one of the best! Another regular at this venue was a Liverpool-based female impersonator called Lily Savage.

I was often booked with strippers, and Sunday lunchtimes in the clubs would often consist of me singing some songs before a variety of ladies, who were advertised as 'exotic dancers' or 'one for the boys', got out onstage to do their thing. I chatted to many of them. Most were housewives who were making extra cash, but I met one girl who was very popular, as she was a bit of a stunner. I found it very odd that her dad came along with her and he seemed to pay great attention to his daughter's performances. At Jumples club in Halifax and later at Chapeltown WMC near Sheffield I clearly heard the father instruct his young daughter to "get out there and be horny" before slapping her on her bottom as the music started and she headed out onstage. I was beginning to realise that if I was going to stick around in the business, I would have to remain unshocked and unperturbed about almost everything.

Bentley snooker club near Doncaster was the first venue where I was physically attacked. My inebriated assailant didn't get very far. In a drunken haze, this silly lad missed me altogether and some local lads physically opened the exit door with his head.

My first Christmas in Clubland consisted of a Christmas Eve gig at Moorthorpe Recreation club near Pontefract and a Boxing Day show at the tiny Moorend club in Cleckheaton near Bradford.

New Year's Eve 1986 saw me entertaining at Blakeborough club in Brighouse near Huddersfield. My father-in-law and mother-in law came along with my wife Melanie on the night. As we were loading my PA equipment in to this pokey and unwelcoming club, a gale force wind shut the van door right on my mother-in-law Kathleen White-head's wrist. My father-in-law Gordon Whitehead took her straight to the local hospital, but the show had to go on.

The show did. The money was a joke, the audience were awful. Was it time to think again about my limited career options and should I persevere with my plans to become the world's greatest entertainer?

*

20

I can't even remember quite how it happened, but I met Stan Hartshorne in 1987 and we became firm friends. Stan was a bachelor who ran a printing business from amazingly down-at-heel premises on the outskirts of Wakefield. He had a Jack Russell dog for company, smoked incessantly and soon become my 'roadie'.

Stan had previously been a roadie and friend of a singer, then only recently retired, called Barry J Douglas. I think Stan loved club life. He was concert secretary of a club in Wakefield and by the time I met him, Stan has launched a local club magazine called *The Wakefield and District Review*. At some point early in 1987 Stan asked me if I wanted to write a column about what was on in the clubs in the local area and that was the very beginning of my sideline as a freelance entertainment writer.

Stan was just plain lucky. He used to win raffles etcetera on a regular basis in many clubs. Where Stan really made waves was with the bingo fans. His habit of winning at bingo used to cause ructions with the club people, many of whom believed that visitors should not be allowed to play. I never played, so to me there was never a problem. In addition, many of the club people sat in exactly the same seats every single concert or bingo night. As entertainers arrive before anyone else to set up equipment onstage, if Stan and I went and sat out front in the concert room, we always knew if we were sitting in someone's regular seat. Some folk would come over and just tell you to move, while others would simply hover tut-tutting whilst standing around and shuffling their feet in quiet indignation. Some clubs got around the problem by reserving seating for visiting artistes. This is seldom a service I avail myself to, as in recent years I simply sit in the dressing room and read or watch DVDs – when not onstage of course. Performing to me has always been just a job and that is what has kept me reasonably sane all these years.

During the early years it occurred to me very quickly that my light-hearted patter was often going down better with the audience than the singing. I started learning a few jokes and gradually worked them into my show. Stan and I did the rounds during 1987 and '88, and some of the venues we visited were unforgettable.

Stan died in 1996 after fighting lung cancer. I was his final hospital visitor and his death was pretty hard to take. I was asked to stand up and speak at Stan's funeral, at St Michael's church in Lower Westgate, Wakefield. I simply said that Stan was a gentleman and a very gentle man without an enemy in the world. Not many men I have known could shuffle off this mortal coil with that sentiment expressed.

A venue in Pontefract was known by the locals by the nickname 'Fraggle Rock'. This was a place where visiting truck drivers and contractors working away from home mixed with the local ladies. The historic town of Ponte-fract still to this day boasts a vibrant night scene and the place is known colloquially as 'Ponte-Carlo'. Fraggle Rock booked live acts every night of the week but the customers were invariably way more entertaining than anything that might be going on onstage. There was seldom any trouble. Brian was the Boss and he owned a huge Alsatian dog and a wife whose disapproving gaze could turn a hard man's legs to jelly in seconds. The most notorious aspect of Fraggle Rock was the sexual shenanigans, which produced some pretty wild nights if truth be told. Fraggle Rock is no more. Nowadays the old premises are now home to a pizza restaurant.

The Midland Road social club in Royston near Barnsley (known locally as 'The Bush') was once a place where my mother had played the piano and organ and accompanied visiting artistes. The club had a proper sprung dancefloor and an ornate glass ceiling, which must have cost a fortune. The place is now an old people's home.

Emley football club near Huddersfield staged an outdoor festival in 1987, in which Gary Glitter was booked to headline the music on the football pitch. I was rather more humbly booked in the evening to provide entertainment for club members in the small adjacent social club. Mr Glitter came in and made a loud and extravagant entrance. He said hello and shook my hand. It has occurred to me in the light of more recent events that perhaps I was just a little too old and the wrong gender group for him to waste too much time of his time on me.

Private functions can be a wonderful source of income

for entertainers but they don't always run smoothly. Organisers are often not accustomed to professional entertainment and sometimes these evenings can be rather ad hoc. At one such event I was booked to perform an hour's cabaret for wedding reception guests. The groom was a bit of a fan of mine and he told me of his ambition to become a stand-up comedian. His kin, seated on one side of the venue were of the rough and ready variety. The blushing bride clearly came from much more genteel stock and her relatives were seated as far away from the groom's people as possible. The groom's plans for the evening included getting on the microphone and performing as my 'warm-up'. With his own raucous relatives on one side and bride's nearest and dearest on the other, the groom began his string of off-colour gags and launched into his comedy debut after having consumed a lot of beer. Immediately after this wedding comedy debacle, I was swiftly introduced onstage. To some extent I managed to leaven the effects of the direction the evening had taken and provide a few songs and a charm offensive for the benefit of the bride's family, many of whom had been tut-tutting their way through the contribution of my impromptu warm-up man.

Looking back, I think perhaps certain members of the groom's family could easily have been part of some right-wing racist group as, after my spot I was met by a delegation of young men who started trying to tell me the type of jokes they reckoned I should have told. They were all jokes about black or Asian people. I was frankly surprised to find their wedding attire did not consist of Ku Klux Klan garb.

I caused panic one night in the Ritchie household when I returned from a booking at a former social club near Bradford. The owner, a stage hypnotist, was trying to get rid of the club as he couldn't control the local ingrates who had infiltrated the place. I was booked for an early spot, so just before leaving, one local lunatic decided me would try and rob me of my fee. I was wearing a pristine white shirt, which was covered in blood when I arrived home. I thought my wife would be in bed and my intention was to sneak in, throw the shirt in the wash and change clothes. My wife was up and around with my daughter Michelle, who was poorly at the time, and looked at me in horror as I walked in looking like I had just returned from a shift at an abattoir. My first wife is a pretty tough lady, but she was relieved when I revealed that the blood wasn't in fact mine and that the moron who attempted to steal my cash had somehow broken his nose during our confrontation and bounced off a wall and straight back into my arms, covering me with claret! I quickly placed this most optimistic and misguided of muggers in the recovery position, told a bloke hanging around the front door to call an ambulance and off I sped.

It dawned on me that I needed to move up a division or two and try and land better quality work or take up judo again. The answer to this seemed to me to be finding a good agent. In 1988 I won a Clubland award and was named entertainer of the year by one of the club federation entertainment sections. The photo, of me grinning inanely, was all over the local papers in Yorkshire and news of my success reached an agent by the name of Les Parker.

*

—21—

During his time onstage Les Parker had been a multi-award-winning Clubland and cabaret entertainer, whose blend of comedy and music made me aspire to be just like him – onstage at least. Les bought a club which was formerly known as Jim Windsor's club in Leeds, before retiring from the stage and concentrating on being an agent. His publicity was emblazoned with rhyming slogans like 'You Need Our Acts to Get Your Clubs Packed' and 'Not a Lot to Pay and We're Here All Day'.

By the time he became my exclusive and sole agent, Les had bought a small cabaret venue and restaurant just outside Wakefield. As a bit of a thank-you, some of us were engaged to perform at his venue for very little by way of financial remuneration. Les used to accept bus parties into the venue, which all came from club customers who would normally be found in club premises situated all over Yorkshire. Along with a singer called Ricky Graham, I used to entertain at most such evenings.

At one evening I met a young woman who I had met only once previously. She had come along with a couple, who turned out to be her mum and dad. This pleasant young lady and I chatted. She told me she had been working in various night clubs as a sales and promotion girl, but her real love was singing. She asked me if she could get up onstage and sing and I thought she certainly had something. After the show I was having a late-night drink with Les and I asked him what he thought of the girl. He replied that he wasn't too keen as he had too many girl singers on his books already.

I managed to change his mind and as it turned out, Les phoned her the following day and asked her to attend an audition night, which was held at Harehills WMC in Leeds. The young lady was nervous, but impressive and Les signed her up on the spot. The singer's name was Jane McDonald and I have read different accounts on how Jane found her first fledgling foothold in Clubland. None of them are accurate. This is in fact what really happened.

By that time, I had met a new friend in Howard Burnette. Howard was an amputee pub-landlord, disc jockey, singer, comedian, entertainer, magician and complete enigma. You always knew exactly where you stood with Howard because he always let you down. Sometimes he let himself down too, but that was his business.

A shared love of Johnnie Walker Black Label whisky and certain narcotic substances bonded our friendship, and by 1988 I was running a talent show called Mark Ritchie's Rising Stars every week at his fun pub, the Alexandra Bar in Wakefield. The venue was later renamed the Out of Town and was the haunt of local villains and other such characters. Howard had a way of dealing with troublemakers. He used to set fire to them.

There were no bouncers employed there. The place was full of them, all local hard men who were devoted to Howard and his family. The setting fire to people was done in the certain way. One huge local bully called Paul

Sykes had spent the majority of his life in prison, but at one time he was a championship contender in the heavyweight division of boxing. Paul was barred from just about everywhere in 1988 but barged into Howard's place one night demanding a drink. The bellowing Mr Sykes stood around 6' 5", while Howard was around 5' 6". Throughout a face-to-chest finger-prodding and bellowing confrontation, Paul didn't seem to notice that Howard was surreptitiously spraying a flammable solution on to his trousers and shoes. A number of professional minders gathered closer just as Howard set Paul's clothing alight. The minders then pushed the walking inferno that was Paul Sykes into the street and he went to hospital suffering from serious burns.

Paul wrote an award-winning autobiography called *Sweet Agony*, and I can't really criticise him as he never did me any harm at all. He died on the streets of Wakefield in 2001, where he had long lived as a vagrant. He was a lost soul.

Howard Burnette moved on to live and work in Benidorm, Spain later on in life, where he finally faced up to his demons before he died in Villajoyosa hospital near Alicante in 2005. Howard had lung cancer. I could tell a million stories about him, but no one would believe most of them!

About that time, I had been approached by my local newspaper *The Wakefield Express* to become their new Clubland writer, after my predecessor, a lovely man called Michael St Claire decided to stand down. Along with three other local newspapers, I submitted a column for each title every week. Rain or shine, poorly or well, on holiday or not for 33 years I kept banging the columns out. When the newspaper became computerised in 1996, we all had to learn new skills, but for many years I bashed away on an old typewriter.

Working in the local press I had begun to garner a certain celebrity status, with my name and face in all the local newspapers and regular spots on BBC radio, the extra money I was earning came in very handy indeed. The problem was at some of my local gigs. Writing a hard-hitting and often controversial column every week, where I was trying to point out some kind of direction that may increase the dwindling numbers of folk venturing through the club doors, while at the same time going onstage and trying to get laughs, made me a real target for some frankly odd people, who seemed to feel a sense of entitlement to dislike me when they sat out front in Clubland audiences many of the members of which were trying their best not to enjoy my act.

With work coming in from all over the place, my diary was fine, but I couldn't fill a phone box in my own home town. Being an outsider in every aspect of my experience thus far was a feature of my life which I was by now well accustomed to. My skin was becoming thicker, but looking back I now know that I must have appeared aloof and even arrogant to people who didn't take the time and trouble to get to know me properly. For me it was about self-preservation.

*

In 1989 I came up with the idea of presenting a charity event which would become an annual cabaret festival type show featuring a multitude of artistes. Painthorpe country club was the venue and a 600-strong audience packed the place. The first-ever show was quite a colourful affair and I was becoming a show producer, having already put together the aforementioned talent show at Howard Burnette's venue. Much to my surprise I had found something I actually had a flair for.

In the meantime, Les Parker was making my work diary bulge with much nicer work than I had previously been accustomed to. Things were going far too well, but a huge spanner was about to be thrown into the works of my life. This self-inflicted wound can be easily described and is surely the world's oldest cliché: I fell in love.

Early in 1989 Les spoke to me about two offers which had come in for summer season work. With an infant daughter and a wife who had only recently gone back to full-time work at the bank, there was a lot to consider and weighing up the pros and cons took quite a while.

The first offer was very easy to deal with and promptly reject. A representative from a huge company had seen me making a rare appearance in the Blackpool area and he reckoned I was just right for a venue within the very beautiful Winter Gardens complex in Blackpool town centre. The job was to be part of a show which would be presented six afternoons and six nights a week in a sort of pub-style music saloon within the complex. I can't remember the money that was mentioned for the job, but the cost of a bed and breakfast would have been factored into the weekly fee which was offered. The numbers seemed derisory to me and simply wouldn't have been worth my while. I turned the job down. The engagement would have been 26 weeks and end only when the famous Blackpool illuminations went dark for the winter.

Parker then rang the guy back to tell him I would not be joining them in Blackpool that summer. His next call was to me and Parker was laughing like a drain down the phone. Les told me amid the guffaws about the 'improved' offer from Blackpool. I was to be informed that would be no increase in money on offer, but I would have my name and face emblazoned on one or more of the famous Blackpool trams. Even with the dubious 'honour 'or cache of seeing my ugly mug traversing up and down from Starr Gate all the way to Fleetwood, had I accepted the job I would not have been able to pay my mortgage or help with childcare etcetera.

The other summer offer came from the Yorkshire coast and the resort of Bridlington, which is situated about equidistant of Scarborough and Hull. This old-fashioned British seaside resort boasts a large harbour and a long promenade which stretches north towards the stately home which was the birthplace of the aviatrix Amy Johnson.

In that year of 1989 licensing hours altered throughout the UK. Pubs, bars and clubs were allowed for the first time to remain open selling alcohol all day long. There was a number of nightclub premises in Bridlington which all offered live shows during the day for the daytrippers and coach parties, as well as catering for holiday-makers during the evening. I was offered a summer season at one such nightclub in return for excellent wages and a 22-week contract. On summer season in the town that year were comedian Norman Collier, the comedy showband Black Onyx and 70s chart-topping glam rock band The Rubettes.

At my nightclub venue, I was to star in and arrange a supporting cast for a show which would be offered on a fairly ad-hoc basis every midweek daytime, Monday to Friday and four evenings a week, Monday through to and including Thursday. In other words, nine shows a week.

I saw it as career advancement and the money was certainly tempting, so I accepted. Despite my beloved daughter being only 21 months old when the job contract began, childcare was arranged and split between a nursery and her maternal grandparents.

By the time we got going properly, the supporting players included two singing and dancing guys, who I named The Symbolics. These guys wore grass skirts and they introduced themselves as 'Sym' and 'Bollics'. On the show there was also an Elvis impersonator called Johnny Presley. Johnny didn't just think he was Elvis, he knew he was Elvis! 'Little Annie' was a large and buxom girl who sang Michael Jackson songs, and the star of the afternoon show was a 78-year-old female stripper who just loved to dance naked.

After 151 performances that season, I was exhausted, my voice was damaged and my marriage was close to foundering on the rocks. The reason was Mandy. She worked behind one of the bars and I fell for her hook, line and sinker.

I could smell Mandy on my clothes. I could taste her in my mouth and my mind was constantly filled with mental images of her. After the season ended, I wrestled with my conscience. I was after all a married man. Due to the already fractured state of my marriage, I am ashamed to admit that the female in my life who was the deciding factor in my ending the romance with Mandy was not my own long-suffering wife. It was my then two-year-old daughter, who I loved and cared about more than anything in the world.

My retentive memory for phone numbers and all manner of numbers for that matter, determined that I could not get Mandy's phone number out of my head and I kept in touch with her from time to time. Given the benefit of hindsight, I know I was merely forestalling the inevitable and stretching out the agony.

During the years which followed, I thought of Mandy often. I wondered how her life had panned out, but did not attempt to contact her for many, many years. My son Steven was born in 1990 and my family unit was complete. The collateral damage to the marriage that is one of the many consequences of an affair which the spouse finds out about, is often immeasurable and leaves deep wounds which are scratched and pried open from time to time. It was entirely my fault. It was my responsibility and the guilty have to take the blame. I carried the guilt around like luggage and the burden became heavier and more cumbersome as the years passed.

By 2003 Melanie had moved out of our marital home, a detached house in Altofts, after my marriage to her had collapsed after 21 years in 2001. I promptly moved back in and decorated it in order to put it up on the market and sell the only recently extended property at 8 Eskdale Croft. I was quite alone in the house one night and I began to think of Mandy. I had not thought of her for any special reason. It was just as if something was gnawing away at my brain and the train of thought would not go away, as I tried in vain to sleep that night.

The following morning, I was driving into Wakefield to collect mail from the newsroom at *The Wakefield Express*. Standing in the usual morning traffic jam on Ferry Lane in Stanley. I picked up my mobile phone and rang the number in Bridlington which I had tried so hard to forget. I recognised the unmistakeable voice of Mandy's mum and lost my nerve, changed my mind and turned my phone off.

All day long the urge to call again would not go away and sometime during the evening, I picked up the phone. Her mum answered again and this time I asked for Mandy. I had not spoken to her mum for almost 15 years, but she recognised my voice immediately. I soon heard the news that rocked me to my core. Mandy was in hospital and whilst being treated for leukaemia, she had suffered a brain haemorrhage on the previous evening and was not expected to survive.

Armed with the mobile number of Mandy's younger sister Jane, I made contact and was invited to come straight over to Leeds general infirmary, where she had been moved to that day and where Jane was sitting at her sister's bedside.

I arrived quite late in the evening and after a welcome hug from Jane, she brought me up to date on Mandy's life. She had married, but the marriage was not a success although it did produce a son. Mandy's husband had left her only a few weeks previously and was therefore not present at the hospital. I saw her unconscious and connected to much hospital apparatus in the intensive care unit. I left in the wee small hours, headed home and wept.

One week later, after daily phone calls, there had been no change to Mandy's condition and she was on life support. I was away on business during that week on the South Coast. By now I was working for the national show business publication *The Stage*, which comes up repeatedly and at length much later on in my story. I was literally floating around and enjoying lunch on a boat, which belonged to my friend, the entertainment agent Ron Martin. Ron is fine company and for a while my thoughts of Mandy were put aside. Whilst cruising just off the Isle of Wight, my mobile phone rang. It was Jane, who was in tears. Jane told me that it had been decided that the consultant in charge of Mandy's care was to visit the following morning and make the decision which everyone had been dreading regarding the removal of life support.

I had business in Dorset that evening and it was decided that I should come straight to the hospital in Leeds, after driving through the night. I finished the job and set off on my long night drive. My car was fast and thanks to an Oxford traffic cop, it became much easier than it should have been. I was stopped for speeding and the policeman asked me to sit in the back of his car. He asked me why I was travelling so fast and he clearly believed my extraordinary story. I could have kissed this wonderful officer of the law, when he told me to get back into my car and follow his blue lights. I only just managed to keep up with him. A further set of blue lights in front turned out to belong to a policeman in a neighbouring county, who accompanied me and effectively cleared my path for a further 60 or so miles.

Thanks to the friendly and speedy cop cars, it took only slightly over three hours to make the journey and I arrived and parked outside the hospital, in the city centre of Leeds around 4am I made my way to the bedside and started to speak to Mandy, who was still unconscious. I told her I loved her and said my goodbyes. She looked exactly as she did all those years before and even had the same hairstyle. Mandy was beautiful and resembled a fragile porcelain figure, I said goodbye and dragged myself off home.

Leaving the hospital, there were just a few early morning people around, before the city had woken up and the streets were still unaired. I drove the few short miles back home and fell into a deep sleep.

An evening phone call from Jane was what I was dreading but to my surprise the call came early in the following afternoon. The consultant surgeon had suggested another method to help Mandy recover from surgery, which was devised to ease the pressure on her brain. The initial signs were good and two months later Mandy was taken home to Bridlington and back into the care of her mother and sister.

Exactly four months after she left hospital, Mandy met me in a hotel bar in Bridlington. The Expanse Hotel stands on the seafront where we used to stroll along together during the summer of '89.

Although her speech was impaired and her movement was limited, Mandy's physical abilities and faculties were returning slowly but surely.

I had no agenda regarding Mandy and no thoughts or aspirations about resuming our romance. My feeling was that was then and this was now.

In any event, by that time I had already met my best friend and second wife, who hates being called Beverley, so most people call her Bev and I dubbed her 'my Bevvy'. We were later to marry in 2011 and we are as happy as clams.

Bevvy loves me just as I am. The result was that I just had to know what had become of Mandy and Bevvy understood this. I am not in touch with Mandy anymore, but I still think of her often. Who knows, perhaps she thinks of me too.

Time to turn the page.

*

—23—

At the start of the 1990s I encountered two big problems. Firstly, Les Parker was dying of cancer and he was schooling his protegé the singer Ricky Graham in the requirements of being an agent and taking over what was then a flourishing business.

A wise old London agent called Kenneth Earle once opined to me that agents who were also entertainers would never ever make it in the agency business as they didn't know what side of the business they were meant to be on. I believe this to be the case with Ricky Graham. Ricky was and remains a great singer and entertainer, who enjoyed pop chart success back in the late 70s in a group called Child. Ricky and I remain good friends to this day, but I just knew that at that time I did not want him to represent me. When Ricky replaced Les, my work suffered, my confidence was flagging and I knew I had to make a change.

Secondly, although I was performing quite a lot of comedy by then, a strong singing voice was still very much a prerequisite to making a living. I was struggling to produce a voice and one night, during a club gig at Sheepscar club in Leeds, my croaking vocal just refused to be produce any kind of noise at all.

Mr Bloomer was the name of an ear, nose and throat consultant who saw private patients at his home in the posh Wakefield suburb of Sandal. Self-employed people don't get paid if they don't work, so waiting around for months on end on a National Health waiting list was never an option. I paid the fee and soon, after a relaxant had been sprayed into the back of my throat, my tongue ended up lolling around on my chin. The erudite Mr Bloomer knew all about singers and their occasional problems in producing a voice. Whilst under his care, he diagnosed I had developed tiny growths known as polyps on my vocal folds. Scraping them off with a scalpel whilst anaesthetised was back then the only option and onto the National Health waiting list I went. Nowadays the procedure is done in seconds and by laser.

I did not sing at all then for around six months, until my operation due date came up and I was saved. After a session or two of speech therapy, a man called Hugh Maynard started to teach me how to use my voice properly and my vocal troubles were largely over.

Back onstage again, I had a new agent. His name was Mike Hainsworth – and Mike ran the Flair Theatrical Agency. Soon my confidence was restored, the quality of the work I was being offered was back on track and I was to be represented by Mike for eight successful years. I left him in 1997, for reasons I shall go in to later. Today Mike's ambitious and conscientious daughter Rachel runs the Flair Agency and we all remain firm friends.

Once back into stage work, I was brought back to earth with a bump early in 1992, when I was subject to an investigation by the tax-gatherers at the Inland Revenue. I'm sure their people expected to find I had hidden untold riches away from their steely and thorough scrutiny. In fact, I ended up with a refund of just over £1,000, as I had apparently overpaid.

Melanie and I booked a holiday on the island of Malta. It was a great holiday, but there was some drama attached to it, when our toddler son Steven was picked up from playing on the beach by a Maltese woman, while we were all relaxing on the neighbouring Island of Gozo, at a town called Marsalforn. I was swimming in the sea with my daughter Michelle, when I saw Melanie running after the woman who was off like a flash, with Steven in her arms. There was a kind of police box on the seafront, where a Maltese bobby was eating a sandwich. Melanie was running and shouting at the policemen simultaneously about the woman sprinting off with our son in her arms.

Observing the scene from my dip in the sea, I scooped up Michelle and gave chase up a sidestreet. The drama soon ended as the policeman stopped eating his sandwich, paced off up the street, where Melanie was already in the doorway of a house. It was soon revealed by the police officer that the woman apparently had an annoying habit of scooping up blonde-haired and blue-eyed boy children and taking them into her home, offering sweets and other treats. She didn't seem to realise the worry and concern she had caused and the woman's apologetic daughter, anxious to make amends, even invited us all to stay for dinner. Melanie was never what could be described as a delicate bloom and she give an admonishment to the woman and her family, which was short, uncomplicated and to the point.

It was then back to the club work and about that time I had some brand-new publicity photos taken in a local studio. I now had come up with a sort of show business soubriquet and my billing was 'Mark Ritchie – The Entertainer'.

The work highlights that year saw me appearing on-stage within the walls of HMP Prison Wakefield, in a show with the great actor and comedian Bobby Knutt, who sadly died in 2019. The prison has earned the nick-name 'Monster Mansion', due to the fact it houses mass-murders, rapists, sex offenders and terrorists. Nowadays the 'screws' and their families socialise in a prison offi-cers' club just outside the walls, but back then the club consisted of a rather dusty hall within the walls and visitors had to pass through a cleverly concealed and integrated door, right in the heart of the prison wall itself. I worked with Bobby, affectionately known as 'Knutty', many times in the ensuing years and I was delighted when he ended up starring in the telly sit-com *Benidorm*.

Mike Hainsworth managed to get me better money then I had earned previously and I was working on aver-age five nights every week. Some of the social club names where I entertained sound like they came out of the script of a sit-com. I was soon strutting my stuff onstage at places such as Malton Bacon Factory club, the Pegasus club, Driffield, the Excelsior Crisps club, Grimsby, the Stocksbridge Legionnaires club, the Royal Antideluvian Order of Buffalos club, Scunthorpe, the Bass Brewery social club, Tadcaster, Brumby and Frodinghams club, Scunthorpe, Little Horton Cycling club, Bradford, the Pop and Pastie club, Keighley, Westborough Ratepayers club, Dewsbury and the Cemetery club, Scunthorpe.

It wasn't the big time, but the pay was good!

*

24

During 1992 and '93, I was invited into some touring shows, including the Vanda Steel Experience. Vanda, largely forgotten these days, was being promoted by her partner, a man we knew as Mick Jones. Soon we were all touring around what remained of the Northern cabaret venues, complete with a troupe of dancers and the shows were a success. Hardly anyone knew, but Mick and Vanda both had drug problems and didn't stick around very long in the business.

I received a call about a booking at West Leeds WMC one day. It was a last-minute call and I was told to expect television cameras when I got there. Armed with little in the way of further information, I arrived at the appointed hour to be met by a researcher/runner from Yorkshire Television, who seemed utterly confused and rather perplexed to find that I had no idea what the evening was all about. Rather flustered, she informed me that I was to provide some entertainment as a warm-up man. She elaborated by explaining that the place would soon be full of 'homosexuals' and the programme was about a spike in cases of HIV and Aids which had cropped up mysteriously in Yorkshire at that time. The first cases of Aids in the UK were several years before, but the hysteria and paranoia regarding the condition was still at its height. Things came to a head as some dissenting voices were heard outside the concert room gathering in the foyer of the club. It seems extraordinary today and per-haps even a little bizarre but I heard people demanding that the HIV patients contributing the telly show should be removed.

I was invited around this time to provide daytime mu-sical entertainment at the Rampton secure psychiatric hospital in Nottinghamshire. A guide took me through a series of gates and I set my sound equipment up in a large hall. The patients were then paraded in, sat down and I began singing songs and throwing in bits of patter. An audience containing the criminally insane was not what I signed up for, but it was certainly an experience. Many of the patients applauded politely before filing out back to whatever constituted their normal lives. My guide than waited until I broke down all my sound equipment and guided me through a labyrinth of doors and gates until I was back to my vehicle and off into the mad world outside.

Brownroyd club in Bradford was a regular venue for me. The venue stood on the edge of the town's red light district. The street at the side of the club contained a dark and secluded warehouse space, where the prostitutes often directed their clients after the men had picked them up by kerb-crawling.

After a gig one night, I was loading my equipment into the car when I noticed a young-looking girl getting out of another car just a few yards away in what I figured was probably post-coital business parking. Keeping a look-out with the corner of my eye, I saw the girl light up a fag and walk up to me, where to my surprise she began to chat. "What have you been doing in there, are you a turn?" The chat developed and she told me of her desire to become a singer and enquired how she could find her way onto the club scene. A long chat followed as I became increasingly intrigued by the nature of the conversation. My new hooker friend seemed very sincere and she told me how desperate she was to get off the streets, as she had recently beaten heroin addiction and had a little money behind her.

I found myself handing her a business card with my number on it and told her to give me a call if she needed any more information. To this day, I have no idea why I did that. She asked if I was married and promised to ring off should my wife answer the phone. I said that wouldn't be necessary and she should just ask for me. The girl then looked at me almost apologetically as she offered to "make it worth my while with a free blow-job". I thanked her but declined the offer.

The very next day the aspiring singer rang me and told me she had an audition with an agent I happened to know and would I like to come to the audition night, which was to be held at a club in Morley near Leeds. I took Melanie along on the night and this tastefully dressed young girl could certainly sing and looked like a complete natural entertainer. The agent signed her up and her career in the clubs lasted a good ten years, before she moved to Spain and purchased a bar on the Costa Del Sol, where she still lives and works today.

A summertime gig during a warm spell at Hightown club near Dewsbury ended bizarrely. With all the club doors and windows propped open, a young girl in the audience who was flirting with me after the show, decided for some inexplicable reason to run up and kiss me and then promptly run away. My mystery kisser then appeared to accidentally kick a wedge which was keeping a door ajar as she disappeared off into the night. A man was standing holding a pint in one hand, while his other hand was in the door jamb, as he leant against the door. The door swung shut and sliced one of his fingers clean off. The man went off to hospital and I went off home.

A few days later my agent Mike Hainsworth received a solicitor's letter informing us I was to be sued in regard to the incident. My solicitor Ian Pollard engaged a private investigator, who visited the club and obtained statements which confirmed that I was not responsible for the accident and that anyone who stands with his fingers in a propped-upon door jamb was, to use a legal expression, 'the author of his own misfortune'. I heard no more about the matter.

The annual Clubland Festival charity show I devised was held at Painthorpe country club near Wakefield that year. The sprawling event featured a cast of Clubland luminaries to match any at the time. The cast list comprised Mick McGinley, Johnnie Martell, Natural High, Vicki Calvert, Mark Stanley, Paul Somers, Sample This, Sammy King, Bobby Diamond, Suzi Lees, Michael France, Jane McDonald, the Muldoon Brothers, Vanda Steel, Bobby Marx, Nikki Landon, Mike Terry, Saddletramp, Neat and Tidy. Sunny Daye, Karen King, Gino and Barry Santana – plus me of course. All of whom were hardly household names, but singer, chart-topping songwriter and comedian Sammy King had toured with the Beatles and Jane McDonald was becoming ever more popular. These huge sprawling affairs raised many thousands of pounds, helping the then newly built Wakefield hospice become established.

Les Parker had only recently died around this time, and his funeral at Lawnswood cemetery in Leeds was attended by many hundreds of mourners. Most of us never even managed to get anywhere near the chapel.

It was like the end of an era and a tribute show was staged in October of 1991 which I was asked to act as compere for. Appearing on the night were singers Diane Peters and Ricky Graham, comedians Peter 'Machine Gun' Wallis, Nicky Newsome and Jim Bowen of TV game show *Bullseye* fame, plus Les' favourite live band Turnstyle. The show was produced by the agent Gordon Kellett.

Things were moving on in the clubs and early the in 90s society was changing, with many homeowners in negative equity, a financial crash looming and technology producing the biggest changes in society since the Industrial Revolution.

*

25

Until the end of my association with my agent Mike Hainsworth at Flair Agency in 1997 the work was often varied, but the fees he managed to obtain for my humble services were always very good.

In 1992 I took my first of many trips to the Spanish resort of Benidorm and appeared on a show with a fascinating character called Roy Jay, who was more widely known as the 'Slither Man'. Roy and I crisscrossed between two cabaret venues, basically performing the same spot twice in venues which were within walking distance of each other. I arrived the night before the month-long engagement was due to start and decided to pop in and sit at the back while Roy was onstage. He always wore a suit which was covered with prison-like arrows and his mannerisms were incredibly funny. Genius is often so close to madness and I know that Roy faced many personal demons during his everyday life. As a live stand-up comedian, he really was special. I laughed so much on that first evening in Spain that I literally fell off my chair!

Another act Mike Hainsworth represented was Dene Michael, who had become part of the infamous party band Black Lace and Dene was by then touring with his own party and function band. I was booked onto a series of shows as supporting act and one evening at a hotel venue in Hull stands out in my memory. Dene is a party animal through and through and I remember he was very kind to my young children when he was entertainment manager at the Flamingoland theme park in East Yorkshire. Dene's on-park accommodation was actually within the confines of a huge zoo at the park. It was very strange drinking our tea in Dene's garden as a herd of elephants trumpeted past. Meanwhile back in Hull it was the annual taxi-drivers' dinner. We were given a hotel room to use and a free food and drinks tab, plus overnight accommodation.

When the tab was presented the following morning, the taxi-driver who had organised the 'do' looked aghast. His face reminded me of what that of a taxi customer would look like if he hadn't realised his driver had left the fare clock ticking during a 20-mile motorway tailback.

Mike Hainsworth organised an annual party for the artistes he represented and this was always held on early January, when work was scarce. Mike had a reputation for tight-fistedness and the party invitation was a classic:

FLAIR THEATRICAL AGENCY ANNUAL CHRISTMAS PARTY AT BRIGHTON STREET CLUB HECKMONDWIKE ON JANUARY 5TH. FREE BAR BETWEEN 8 AND 8.05PM. PLEASE RSVP SO WE KNOW HOW MANY DRIPPING AND MUCKY FAT SANDWICHES TO ORDER!

My lifetime love affair with the island of Tenerife had already begun a few years earlier while Melanie was expecting our first child Michelle. Tenerife is a two-faced island, with a huge volcano Mount Teide causing the weather anomaly of a cloudy and cool area in the north of the island and clear blue skies in the south. In over 30 years of visiting and relaxing on this the largest of the Canary Isles, I have seen it grow and develop. When I visit the place today, Beverley and I favour an area called Costa Adeje. I remember when the San Eugenio area where we stay these days wasn't even there. The area was then occupied by a lone hotel, surrounded by a beach and acres of lunar-like volcanic rocks. Tenerife also comes up again towards the end of my story

Another notable booking around 1993 was staged in Hyde near Manchester within the function room of a public house. A brewery had been persuaded to sponsor the evening, at which civic dignitaries and other pillars of the community were raising funds for a new health centre and its equipment. I was introduced to man called 'Fred', who I was informed was a GP who would be placed in charge of the new health centre once it opened. During the evening it was part of my job to introduce him on to the stage, so 'Fred' could address the packed house of fundraisers. My announcement was very simple: "Ladies and Gentleman, please welcome your friend and mine, Doctor Harold Shipman." The biggest mass murderer in UK history committed suicide in his cell at Wakefield Prison in January 2004 and the rest, as they say, is criminal history.

In April of that year there was a close encounter with a large group of very inebriated and saucy ladies, who worked at the Lyons bakery near Barnsley. Their company had organised a big function at the town's civic theatre. I was fortunate to escape with my trousers still on!

I had performed at the Rudgate and Thorp Arch prison officers' club on many occasions. When a date at this venue was passed to me yet again, I just turned up expecting nothing out of the ordinary. The prison itself has an open section and I was only told on arrival that on this occasion I would be entertaining a group of prisoners who were due for release. I remember going down very badly with the old lags, many of whom looked as though watching my act was only just preferable to a spell in solitary confinement.

Thanks to Mike I landed a brewery roadshow which would see me touring all over the place every Monday through Thursday. Silk Cut was a duo whose husband and wife members consisted of Dave and Linda Major and they too were on the show. Keyboard player Dave and then pregnant singer Linda and I appeared together 101 times. On the very last date Linda went into labour onstage whilst performing and covering a song made famous by the American rock band Heart. Given Linda's condition, the song title makes me laugh out loud to this day: 'All I Wanna Do Is Make Love to You'.

I was roped into some charity work to build a diabetic centre in Wakefield in 1993. Edna Coates was the driving force of the entire project and her friend was the then *Wakefield Express* editor Don Slack. Due to my work in aid of the centre, I was invited to the grand opening do. To officially open the venue, they had invited the Rt Hon

Tom Sackville, who was then health minister. Always referred to in the left-wing press at the time as 'Tory Tosser' Tom Sackville, this man was the Boris Johnson of his day with a bumbling style and a posh boy persona.

This Old Etonian made the mistake of patronising me by singling me out personally and informing me that it was indeed "quite wonderful" to be raising funds for the NHS instead of the government having to fund the service themselves. My response was not exactly polite. My editor Don actually found my encounter with Sackville amusing, later informing me that he couldn't have put it better himself. Sackville left politics in 1997. I'm not sure what he does to fill his time these days but, based on the impression he made on me during my one and only encounter with him, I imagine this chap spends much of his time whipping servants and fox hunting.

In that year I started travelling to Germany to entertain the troops, and the agent over there was a lovely man called Steve Fisher. Fisher was a soldier and a sort of part-time impresario. He lived in an idyllic village called Wamel, which was between Dortmund and Munster and the very first time I went there was for just three nights.

The first night was a regimental disbandment at a large barn just outside the small town of Bad Sassendorf. This was a bit of a rowdy disaster of an evening, but things improved on the second night when I was booked for an after-dinner speech at the sergeants' mess in Buller Barracks just outside Munster. The final night was another sergeants' mess, this time performing in cabaret for the soldiers and their wives and girlfriends at Neiden

Bergheim near the town of Soest, where we also lodged.

I say 'we' as my friend John Law came along with me. John was just recuperating from open heart surgery and after completing the three nights, we drove through the night back to the port of Ostend in Belgium, in order to link up with the ferry to Dover. The fuel pump broke in my van and John and I were stuck sitting in a freezing cold vehicle on a motorway just outside Eindhoven in Holland during the wee small hours of the night. A Dutch AA helped out, but the pump they fitted had to be hooked up to the headlights and wouldn't release enough fuel into the carburettor to go very much over 50mph. We finally arrived back in Yorkshire late on the following evening and John thankfully survived the experience and came through unscathed. He and I were very close and he was the godfather to my son Steven. John's weak heart finally gave out in 1999 and he died in hospital.

Christmas Eve was a great favourite of mine for quite a few years during the 90s, as I appeared on consecutive 'Eves' at the Old Bank club in Mirfield, which is a mill town situated near Dewsbury. The Salvation Army brass band always attended – the sound of Christmas carols being played by a brass band is one of my favourite sounds in the world

*

26

Year after year, through the 90s the kids were growing up fast and I was mainly in charge of their daytime upbringing. Melanie was a high-flyer in banking and was soon managing her own branch in the nearby town of Rothwell. My daughter was experiencing horrendous dental problems and there were dozens of visits to a private orthodontist in Leeds. My son was having hearing difficulties and he had grommets fitted in his ears to counter a condition called glue ear.

The UK property market was in disarray and Melanie and I put a speculative offer in for a large detached house which was only a stone's throw from our home at the time. The previous owners of the house at 8 Eskdale Croft, Altofts had clearly fallen into financial problems and the house was repossessed. Our crazy low offer was accepted and we even had an extension built on to the back of the property.

A chance meeting with a man called Peter Hepple in 1994 was to change things immeasurably in my business life. Peter had been the distinguished and erudite editor of *The Stage and TV Today* in London from 1972 to '92 and had now 'retired' to become the newspaper's consultant editor. We met at the final of a talent show event in my own local area. I was there to help judge the aspiring professional entertainers, who had managed to reach the final of this event. I was also reporting for the local newspapers. Peter was writing a review for *The Stage and TV Today*. Seated together we chatted in between the acts. I had no idea at the time, but I learned later that I was actually being interviewed for a job at the newspaper.

I was visibly tiring as a live performer at that time – through sheer overwork I was often jaded and there was simply nowhere else to go in terms of career advancement with the business contracting year on year.

I started to receive cruise ship cabaret offers. I hated the work and all the hanging around in airports, but I kept looking in that direction for work on and off for much of the period. My agent Mike Hainsworth was very good at obtaining corporate entertainment gigs and sometimes the fees were excellent. My diary records indicate that I was booked for boatloads of well-paid work for a company called Walkers Bingo. There were also a multitude of gig dates which came from the likes of Clarks Shoes, Marks & Spencer and the car company Mitsubishi.

Working in a chain of clubs in the Hull area always made we smile. The punters in all of these clubs were linked by shortwave radio to the bingo caller and they all played the same game of bingo for massive cash prizes. The bingo-person in each club would be armed with a hooter to signal that someone at one of the clubs had called BINGO! and as a result had won a lot of money. Amongst this chain of bingo and social clubs were the Piper club, the Inglemire club, the Belmont club, Southcoates club, the Cherokee club, the Embassy club, the Regency club and Dee Street club. I worked them all. There was a sense of high drama if any of the radio equipment malfunctioned. I also saw many a punter in a state of high dudgeon if they considered that the bingo players in any of the other clubs were winning too often.

Memorable gigs during the mid-90s was many and varied. I was booked on a show by a certain brewery into a venue called the Mosborough miners' club just outside Sheffield. I was appearing alongside Paul Derek, the 'Birdman of Magic'. Paul and his avian menagerie would all arrive in a sort of huge birdcage on wheels. Owls, doves and even crowing roosters appeared everywhere by magic and Paul put so much effort into the magic show, which was only matched by the care and welfare he lavished on his feathered friends.

After Paul's spot, it was incumbent on me to try and follow him onstage and pick up the cabaret baton. Behind the tabs, Paul was collecting, tidying, breaking equipment down and putting the birds back in their travelling accommodation. I was paddling around onstage, virtually up my ankles in bird excrement. I'm sure Paul must have been feeding his birds with Indian food. I told a story which had the attention of the crowd but, just as I reached the punchline, a rooster appeared beneath the curtain, saying hello with a loud cock-a-doodle-doo. I've heard of 'getting the bird', but that was ridiculous!

Intake social club in Doncaster is a club where I have never been well-received despite many gigs there over the years. I was pitching some comedy at the crowd one evening and a huge section of the audience never cracked a smile. After the spot, one of the members of the resident band told me that Intake was the only club in the area where huge bingo screens were used where the numbers appeared immediately as they were called. This facility enabled members of a local society of the deaf to become club members and play the game. As it transpired my perception of their collective indifference to my act was false. A 'heads up' from someone at the club before I went on would have been nice.

A booking at a venue on the Yorkshire coast during the mid-90s was revealing and shocking in equal measure. The venue owner was a successful foreign business man who had married an English lady and they chose to live in and run a pub and hotel. The boss man had gone away for a few days on business the week before my appearance. During his absence another entertainer had turned up as arranged to perform at the venue. This jolly singer and comedian had stayed overnight after the show and taken full advantage of the free drinks on offer. The story goes that this very well-known entertainer had decided to take advantage of the boss man's temporary absence by trying to seduce his wife. Going walkabout during the night, the entertainer made his way into the bedroom of the boss man's horrified wife, who woke to find the entertainer standing naked next to her bed. On the night of my visit to this venue, the boss man asked me various questions about this particular entertainer, after ascertaining that I knew him quite well. Eventually he filled me in on the full details of the previous incident and went on to tell me that he hadn't at that stage decided what an appropriate response should be. Knowing the boss man's reputation and underworld connections, I managed somehow to mollify him. I firmly believe this is the only reason why the aforementioned entertainer is still alive, or at least still attached to his own kneecaps.

I launched the Northern Startrail talent show in the mid-90s and Samsons club near Wakefield was the venue. The owner of the club was former rugby league star David Sampson and his son the fellow rugby league star Dean was also a partner in the club business and was known then as 'the hardest man in the super league'. My business association with the Sampsons would go on for eight successful years and start the careers of many new professional entertainers. We invited my new friend Peter Hepple along to judge the final and I was delighted when he agreed to appear. The winner on the first year was a singer called Sue Drake. Sue soon became known as Susannah Dee and would she would later become a pop star in her own right as part of the chart band Saint.

I was firmly established on the so-called Manchester club scene, where entertainers would appear in two venues every night. I met comedian Bernard Manning at the Embassy club in Harpurhey, Manchester. Bernard owned the place and I never met an entertainer who was so hated and vilified when the reality of his true nature was that of a kind and thoughtful man, who tried very hard to introduce me to what he thought were "the right kind of people". I was booked in to some Sunday shows at his club and after my spots, Bernard would walk on-stage and instruct the audiences: "Don't clap too much, he's from Yorkshire, so the bastard will want more money!"

The clubs in the mill towns of Yorkshire and Lancashire were disappearing fast by the 90s. One of the main reasons was surely that the indigenous white population in many such areas was being rapidly replaced by Asian families, the vast majority of who were not interested in the social club scene. These families have built up a multitude of businesses, some of which operate out of former club premises which were often acquired for a song, having gone bust due to lack of interest from sufficient numbers of the people by then living in the area.

A well-known gangster family in the Yorkshire area owned a cabaret venue which was the haunt of some very bad people. I was booked one night at the venue and the occasion was memorable for all the wrong reasons. I was asked to appear in a 45-minute set, along with Irish comedian Jimmy Cricket. I have no idea how Jimmy went with the crowd that night because I was in my car and escaping straight after my spot. The DJ at the venue had addressed the audience with some kind of in-joke which I didn't understand but was clearly at the expense of the birthday boy. The response was quite shocking. The owner and several henchmen promptly went up to the DJ box and dragged the man into a storage room. I went on to what remained of an audience as many had headed for the exits in droves. As I hurriedly packed some bits and pieces into my car, I beheld the DJ propped up by a mate of his and staggering off home covered in blood and torn clothing.

Various stress-related conditions started to become part of my life. One of them a bowel condition called ulcerative colitis. I endured a spell of surgery in 1995 at the private Methley Park hospital near Leeds. Melanie and the family as a whole benefited from the perk of private hospital treatment due to her status as a bank manager.

Peter Hepple had been in touch regularly, asking me to contribute to a regular light entertainment round-up in *The Stage*. I was asked to attend a show featuring comedian Bob Monkhouse and the venue was Batley Variety club. This iconic cabaret venue had by then changed its name to the Frontier club. I was excited about the new reviewing responsibility I had been entrusted with. On the afternoon of the show I received a phone call: "Hello, Bob Monkhouse here. Would you be interested in meeting up for a drink before the show tonight?" I was delighted. This master stand-up comedian and I met in an adjacent bar about an hour before the curtain was due to go up in front of a packed house in Batley. I asked Bob, who had at the time just celebrated his 65th birthday, why he was interested in the review and, for that matter, my opinion of him. Bob replied perhaps rather tartly: "I'm not. It's just that I collect all my crits and *The Stage* newspaper is world-renowned!"

The after-dinner work kept coming in and one night at Todmorden cricket club sticks out in my mind. Normally at such functions, there would maybe be a sporting speaker and a comedian engaged to provide the entertainment. On this evening a charming and witty man called David 'Rooster' Roberts started the ball rolling. Rooster was then physiotherapist for the England

Cricket Squad. After a sparkling speech of about 20 minutes duration, Rooster gave way for a well-known umpire who stood up and droned on for almost an hour about the interpretation of the LBW rule. There was a lot of alcohol being consumed by the cricket fans, who were by then flagging and nipping out for many and repeated 'comfort breaks'. The captain of the club then piped up and insisted on making his own speech where he told off-colour stories about his mates which no one but the mates themselves understood.

It was then the turn of the main speaker of the evening. His name was Frank Tyson and he used to play for England at cricket back in the 50s. Tyson was nicknamed the 'Typhoon' due to the speed of his bowling. Even after three previous speakers, the Typhoon blew in with a speech which last for way over one solid hour. Many of the more drunk attendees had by then slumped, with many actually falling asleep at the table and using their arms as makeshift pillows. As I surveyed the scene, I knew I had to make a decision as I was being asked to finish off the jollity. I told a couple of stories for the benefit of those who were actually still awake before tip-toeing outside and heading for my car. Thankfully I had been paid in advance.

I agreed a good pay deal from *The Stage*. I was often referred to as 'Our Man in the North' and was also earning bits and pieces from writing reviews for them too. Sometimes reviewers came to my shows and turned the tables on me. In 1996 a great and learned man called Roger Holmes came along to see me at the East Dene club in Rotherham. The place was packed and the show went well. Roger and I remained good friends until his death in 2018.

In 1996 I was booked into sporting dinners with Leeds United legend Norman Hunter and ex-Manchester United manager Tommy Docherty. Tommy, aka the 'Doc', had played in the same team at the legendary Sir Tom Finney and for a time had managed a Manchester United team which featured the great George Best. During a post-speech Q&A, Tommy was asked if he could sign either Finney or Best, which would he sign? His reply was a classic. In an instant he shouted: "Finney – not because I think he was any better than Best but at least he always turned up!"

*

27

In 1997 I met a TV producer by the name of John Dickinson, who needed my help. John needed someone who lived in the Yorkshire television area to help him scout locations for a telly show called *Maynard's Bill*. The show featured actor and former entertainer Bill Maynard touring around what remained of his old haunts in Yorkshire and showcasing the talents of some of the present-day entertainers. Bill was gregarious and kind. He could talk a glass eye to sleep and he loved to corner me and tell me hundreds of his show business stories. I spoke to Bill on the phone shortly before his death in 2017.

By then, due to my new found status as 'Our Man in the North' for *The Stage*, I was receiving quite a bit of telly interest. There was my appearance in a Channel Four docu-soap called *The Entertainers*, which was filmed in the Newcastle upon Tyne area. Then through a new colleague at *The Stage*, Colin Findlay, I became involved in talent-spotting for a new ITV Saturday night primetime Jonathan Ross vehicle, *The Big Big Talent Show*.

In 2008 Melanie and I were entrusted with organising charity events for his worship the mayor of Wakefield. In the mayoral hotseat that year was Councillor Norman Hartshorne, who I first met at Nostell Colliery where he was union secretary for the national union of mineworkers. Norman was simply one of the finest men I ever met.

I had also managed a little more telly exposure working alongside Bill Maynard in the live music-based *Maynard's Bill*.

The same year I was booked to act as producer and compere for the Showcall Showcase, organised by *The Stage* newspaper and at that time the largest trade showcase of light entertainment staged anywhere in Europe. Over a few days and evening sessions bands and all manner of performers were afforded the opportunity to perform short spots in front of anyone and everyone on the light entertainment scene, thereby potentially filling work diaries for the following year. The first Showcall Showcase I was involved in as compere was staged at the Ribby Hall holiday centre near Blackpool. Later on, I moved with the show to compere at the Horseshoe Bar on Blackpool's famous Pleasure Beach. I was presented with a team that I didn't want and would much rather have brought my own people in to work with me, but those were the cards I was dealt.

I changed agents about this time, jumping ship from Flair Agency and letting Gordon Kellett fill my diary. Mike Hainsworth at Flair had only recently bought a skate park in order to capitalise of the new craze of skateboarding. His interest in the agency seemed to have diverted to his new business and my diary was suffering. Business was business after all.

Gordon Kellett was irascible, brusque and tactless, but he was the most honest (often brutally honest) agent in the North and had been in business since 1968. Gordon and I just clicked. We understood each other and that was enough for me. His wife Joan is a lovely lady with impeccable manners and a kind heart. Gordon continued as my agent until his death in 2016.

The year ended on New Year's Eve when I was booked at a small club near Dewsbury. I was sent home early as there was no one left in the club by 11pm, due to the mother of all blizzards piling up outside. I skidded home through the Arctic blast, taking over three hours to travel 16 miles. The year had been busy and lucrative with a touring old-time music hall taking a company of us to small theatres in Hull, Hornsea, Withernsea and Hedon.

An old friend from Nostell colliery days was Roy Greatorex. A genuine eccentric, Roy was mad about the music of Mick Jagger and the Rolling Stones and decided to organise a reunion of Nostell miners ten years after the pit had closed. Roy and his band played Stones hits and his impression of Jagger was spot-on. A few of us got together at the former miner's welfare club, which was by then functioning as a community centre and a great night was had by all, in a show Roy dubbed 'Coaldust in Their Eyes'. Great fun!

As a journalist/reviewer I was beginning to notice how far comedy styles had changed, particular on the night that I saw comedian Mark Thomas for the first time. Thomas reminded me of American comedians I had only seen on film, such as Lenny Bruce and Bill Hicks. The difference was the material, which was all about 'bigging up' socialists and denigrating socialites.

The Clubland Festival of 1997 again raised a fortune for charity and starred Jane McDonald, Stephanie Dooley and Terry Webster, an impressionist who had found fame previously alongside Freddie Starr in a TV show called *Who Do You Do*.

The Showcall Showcase was then run in two segments and a wonderful character called Tufty Gordon acted as compere at the other event, which was staged in Stratford-upon-Avon. Some great times were enjoyed at Stratford with nightly high-jinks at the Swan hotel often going on throughout the night

In 1996 I was summoned to London for lunch with the management of *The Stage*. We lunched at the side of the Thames at a restaurant situated at Shakespeare's Globe Theatre. My role at *The Stage* was formalised and although still technically freelance, I was afforded the official title of 'regional representative'. The title to me sounded more like a salesman than a writer.

The MD was Catherine Comerford and she always struck me as enigmatic. On the one hand Catherine was and I'm sure still remains thoughtful and generous but at times she could be quite child-like and capable of cynicism. Catherine always reminded me of the actress Miranda Richardson and her portrayal of Queen Elizabeth I in *Blackadder*.

In 1998 my beloved Barnsley football club were promoted for the first and thus far only time to the Premier League. Our top-flight odyssey lasted for just one season, but the promotion day, when we defeated Bradford City 2-0 at Oakwell, was one of the happiest times of my life.

*

28

My father-in-law Gordon Whitehead had been ill for some time and in the October of 1999 this kindly and hard-working man died in hospital. We received the news early one morning and Melanie was so upset that I broke the news to the children, who were both heartbroken. It was my job to deliver keys and other security devices to Melanie's staff members at the branch she was the manager of in the nearby town of Rothwell.

Driving on the way back home, I swerved, narrowly missing a car which had just struck a bus. I jumped out to see if I could assist and the driver of the car was clearly in shock, his facial expression frozen, as he grasped the steering wheel. An ambulance was called and several bus passengers had also received minor injuries, but things could have been a lot worse, as the car driver, who I learned from the Pontefract hospital ID pinned to his suit lapel, was a doctor and he had left the ignition in the car sparking, meaning the car was potentially about to explode. I managed to disconnect the seatbelt and, with a mixture of brute force and ignorance, I managed to extricate the good doctor from the wreck and his life was saved. An off-duty nurse who also stopped to attend the scene, had been insistent the man should not be moved until a spinal board arrived. I got my way, as I opined loudly that a spinal board would be no good if he was burnt to a crisp. I was also acutely aware of the heat, the fumes and the fire, not to mention the danger we were all in. After lifting the doctor from the flames and placing him on the heathland ground nearby, the car duly exploded, bang on cue as the expression goes. I gave my name and address to a police officer at the scene, but I never heard anything about this incident again. I then had to go home, get bathed and let my children know about the death of the lovely hard-working man they used to refer to as 'Grandad Brown Bread', due to a song he used to sing to them.

The theme of death continued the week after, as right at the start of a Wednesday show at a club in Heckmond-wike, a lady dropped dead right at the front of the stage. I had learned about CPR techniques years before and I jumped off the stage and gave CPR while the ambulance was on its way. The paramedics arrived very quickly indeed, but they soon gave up and the evening's show was abandoned, with the lady's body being taken away.

My fee for the evening was passed to me in an envelope and I think distracted by the shock of the situation I put the cash in my pocket and headed home. The following day a representative of the club told my agent that I would not be welcome in the club ever again as I had accepted my fee and the feeling was that I should have returned it. I sent the money back through the post, informing the club secretary that I would not be accepting any future work at the club even if it was offered.

Four days later I appeared onstage at a club in Leeds where a man suffered a heart attack right at the foot of the stage. The man died shortly afterwards in the ambulance, but this time the club chairman asked me to resume the show and get onstage as soon as possible. After what had occurred only a few nights before in Heckmondwike, I could not believe what was happening. Most of the audience had gone home or were on their way to the exits by the time I tried to resume my show. It was made abundantly clear to me that I should perform my entire act.

On New Year's Eve it was of course Millennium Night and there was a multitude of reports circulating that entertainers were profiteering and asking for hugely inflated fees. I decided to duck out of the whole shooting match and told my agent that I was not available for work that night. My intention was to go to a party and see in the new century.

About six weeks before the big night, my agent rang to inform me that Wetherby and District social club wanted to book me. I replied that I had no intention of getting into a fee bidding war with anyone. My agent replied, informing me that the club had £1000 in cash if I would agree to appear. My reply was short and simple: "What time do they want me?"

*

29

A new millennium had dawned and I was the wrong side of 40 and faced with the realisation that the clubs, which had formed such a large and important part of my life, were sinking on the mire with the throes of a slow and certain death in front of so many of them. On January 7th 2000 I walked out onstage at a club which had 350 seats in its concert room. A headcount revealed just 44 patrons seated out front.

For many years I had been booked to perform one-nighters at the many Haven holiday camps up and down the country. The work was regular and reliable, but all the cabaret rooms were family orientated and I had to alter my act to make allowances for the children in the crowds and what they wanted and expected in terms of live cabaret. Adult-only holiday centre rooms were becoming increasingly rare, but in 2000 I was booked into a great room at Thornwick Bay holiday centre, which is situated close to picturesque Flamborough Head in East Yorkshire. This place was then privately owned and boasted a large family cabaret room and a neighbouring adult-only venue. Little did I know on that first show that I would form an association with the place which would last 15 years.

In the meantime, the family holiday centre work kept coming, and one night at the Golden Sands park on the Lincolnshire coast saw me falling into a bear-trap. I was told I wouldn't be going onstage until 10pm as there was a talent show final, which they would grateful if I would help with the judging of. Two of the singing contestants were receiving the vociferous vocal support of two factions, presumably consisting of friends and relatives. There could only be one winner and the proverbial hit the fan once the result was announced. The room instantly resembled that of a Wild West saloon as a huge mass brawl broke out. I was quickly ushered onto the stage and walked out to what remained of a crowd, many still sniping across the room at others on neighbouring tables. There was broken furniture, crying children and my 45-minute spot seemed to last forever.

On the health front there was more bowel surgery and throughout the entire time I was confined to a hospital bed, all I could worry about was the money I was losing due to cancelled work. As ever, I was virtually skint and had started to ask Melanie why I always had so little, when I earned so much. I even had a huge overdraft facility on my two bank accounts and the credit cards were out of control.

Don Slack had died in 2000 and he was replaced as editor at *The Wakefield Express* by a great bloke called Neil Speight. I knew Neil's family well as his niece Joanne Speight has been a close friend of mine for most of my life. The only downside of Neil's appointment was that he brought in a reporter called Richard Clarkson. Richard had come from a coal-mining background and wrote a book about the great miners' strike, which I have a copy of, called *Striking Memories*. For some reason I found Richard needling and hostile towards me. He kept turning up for work with a bright yellow pallor to his face and it was clear his alcohol consumption was way out of control. Richard committed suicide in 2001.

On the reviewing front the assignments were coming in thick and fast, but I began to doubt my own judgement whenever I was sent to see some of the more modern comedians, many of who were still proudly declaring themselves to be 'alternative'. To me it all seemed like we were watching comedy performed by students or ex-students. A trip to Barnsley civic theatre was particularly depressing. I chose to sit upstairs and watch a comedy club style evening. A selection of people came and went, none of them were, in my view, stand-up comedians. They were what I call stand around comedians, throwing material around and waiting to see if any of the crap they were throwing at the audience actually stuck thereby producing a laugh or two. In the main the audience were not buying what they were selling, with one particular character by the name of Charlie Cheese faring the worst.

The under-grad style of humour had become firmly established as the way to go for UK stand-up comedians. The comedians seemed to me to be trying to educate and indoctrinate their audiences into their view of what they, the audience, should or should not laugh at. They were and remain to this day, the only type of comedy performers who can secure valuable television exposure and I left the show in Barnsley feeling empty, desolate and irrelevant.

The following evening saw me back onstage and

appearing on a show featuring Charlie Williams. Charlie had been in my dad's class at school and he was one of the UK's first ever successful black comedians. Charlie had funny bones and comparing Charlie's performance with most of what I had grudgingly sat through the evening before was like moving from the ridiculous to the sublime.

An old friend and supporter of mine was Les Sutcliffe. This club official and magazine columnist booked me for his birthday party in 2000, where I appeared with my great friend Tony Wayne. Tony, a fine tenor singer, who I referred to much earlier in this story, will appear again at length later. He was known for giving very long spots and as we left the stage at almost 1am, I said goodnight to the audience by thanking them for spending what must have felt like most of the entire month of May with us!

Another television appearance also cropped up in 2000 on a BBC entertainment documentary called *Made in Manchester*. I was unhappy with the way the show was edited, but the allocated late-night slot the show received suggested that the show has gone by largely unnoticed by the viewing public.

The Stage threw a summer party every year in Blackpool which was attended by any live performers appearing in Blackpool at the time. That year the attendees included Kid Creole, Roy Walker, Bradley Walsh, Joe Pasquale and that rudest of rude comedians Roy Chubby Brown. This was a great event back then and for *The Stage* this was a huge flagship opportunity to meet the light entertainment folks.

I recorded an album of songs, which I began to sell at my gigs on cassette tapes. Nowadays, I still have all five of the albums I recorded over a 12-year period and they are now of course on CD: *Mark One*, *Mark's Other One*, *Mark Ritchie sings the 80s*, *Mark Ritchie sings the 90s* and *Laughs & Lyrics*. Due to streaming it seems that even CDs are largely superfluous to the needs of modern music lovers. Technology moves on and on!

By 2000 the Clubland Festival show was staged for the final time at Samsons club in Wakefield. This would be last of these great flagship cabaret events. Tickets were becoming increasingly tough to sell, as Clubland generally continued on a downward spiral. We certainly went out in style as appearing on the night were singers Stephanie Connah Cole, Tony Wayne and Keith Davidson, plus Elvis impersonator Steve Preston, magician Howard Burnette, singing duo Two Steps Forward, vocal group Soul Story, tribute show the Bacardi Spice Girls and a young lady who was then known as Shauna Phillips. Nowadays 'Shauna' is known as Siobhan Phillips and is an amazing singer, comedienne and musician. Today, despite a high-profile recent appearance in one of the Simon Cowell telly talent-show vehicles, the brilliant Siobhan is possibly the greatest virtually unknown star this country has ever produced. Siobhan is just special. She is funny, she is a great, great talent. Seeing talent like hers wasted, squandered and kept out the spotlight by the strange creatures who run 'Planet Television' sometimes makes me feel utterly depressed.

Describing modern television once, the great Yorkshire comedian Billy Pearce opined that "they (the television people) have taken the show out of showbusiness". Billy is bang on the money. Regarding the viewing audience, the university educated are entertained by other ex-students while, for everyone else, there are celebrity shows and the dubious talents of Keith Lemon. No wonder so many people take anti-depressants these days!

*

30

Late in 2000 I had met a large and jovial man called Ian Sandy while I was covering the Showcall Showcase in Stratford-upon-Avon for *The Stage*. This extremely well-connected show business professional had risen to fame during the 90s due to a successful TV series called *The Seasiders*. Ian was an actor, a producer and a brilliant generous dreamer, with close connections to huge show business companies such as the pantomime giant Qdos.

In February of 2000 Ian made the journey from Brum up to Yorkshire and met me for dinner. A new business relationship was forged between us that night. For the next ten years, until his tragically premature death just before Christmas 2012, Ian became my close confidante, a benefactor and one of the few people I could truly trust.

Those wondering why I dedicated this book to Tommy Brooks may wonder exactly who Tommy Brooks was. I have no idea if he is alive or dead now, but when I first met Tommy in 2000, he was resident compere at the Ravine club in Wigan.

As the new millennium swung into some sort of a rhythm I was still pushing on, looking for the big earner, the main chance, the big opportunity. I was however displaying huge red warning lights within my personality and demeanour. During my appearance at the Ravine, Tommy and I chatted backstage, along with the club's resident musicians. At the turn of the century, so many entertainers were assessing their options, as the live work scene continued to dry up and the only true cabaret/ theatre stages were on board luxury cruise ships. I remember trying to wax lyrical, with my optimistic, homespun homily that: "Live entertainment would never die etcetera." Tommy looked right at me with tears in his eyes and exclaimed: "Can't you see? We're dinosaurs!"

I thought about his words all the way home, across the Pennines and back to Yorkshire. Tommy was right. I was working in a business which was falling apart before my very eyes. I thought of my parents' involvement in Club- land, my teen years in the club bands, the atmosphere gen- erated by all the great performers I had seen. All the best acts I had seen that ever walked the Clubland stages – Dukes and Lee, Harmony Blend, Charlie Williams, John- nie Casson, Paddy Green and all the rest.

A huge black tent of depression enveloped me and seemed to be squeezing the life out of me. I had two growing children who at that time trusted and needed me. That was the first low point of the new century, but there was worse to come.

I felt I was losing my judgement when I was in reality losing my mind and any semblance of control in terms of my own emotional outbursts. My sense of injustice, anger, sadness and generally feeling sorry for myself made me hate what I had become.

The sense of failure was acute and all-consuming and the next show I devised, produced and appeared in was *A Journey Through the Musicals*, a sort of songs from the shows-type offering. The show was a flop. Previously I had just seen an extraordinary 'West-End Wendy' type performer called Robert Bastion at a show in Ross-on-Wye, Herefordshire. I invited Robert up north to appear in a series of shows alongside some fine Yorkshire singers such as Tony Wayne, Michaela May and Vicki Calvert. The show just didn't work somehow.

The talent show I produced and compered at Samsons club began again in the March of 2000, and on one of the early heats, I saw the eventual winner that year, a singer called Julie Reed Asquith – who was certainly in the wrong place at the wrong time in her own life. Julie had a small child from a previous relationship, she was truly outstanding, with a brilliant diva-style voice and stage skills which indicated she was a complete 'natural'.

The Northern Startrail was the name of the show and there was in excess of £2000 in prize money at stake. I was compere and at various periods I was assisted by Billy J Franks, Danny Andrews, Joy Lorraine, Trevor Tunnicliffe and the wonderful lighting technician Roger Auty. The place was packed to the doors every week and kind people who became friends and supporters told me the show was indeed a great event. Peter Hepple wrote in *The Stage*: "This event sets the bar and provides a benchmark for how all stage talent shows should be staged." Praise indeed!

The year also saw me being invited by actor and comedian Ricky Tomlinson to join a short theatre tour of his, which called *Laughter – My Arse!* The show visited some great theatres and the sell-out crowds enjoyed the first run immensely. When the show was repeated in 2002, I was again invited to join the new cast.

I began to feel very anxious and preoccupied with my own personal safety, both at home and whilst travelling around the country on business. 'Throbber' was by then my 'roadie'. His name is Bob Mellor and I dubbed him Throbber due to the regular bouts of gout he endured, during which time his big toes would throb uncontrollably.

Throbber was huge and did not suffer fools gladly, as he proved one evening after a club gig in St Helens. Some lads had broken my car window and were rifling around the inside of my car, until they saw me and ran. I gave chase, but Throbber was at the opposite end of the narrow passageway where the robbers were attempting to escape. One lad jumped at Throbber with fists and feet flying and he was downed and rendered unconscious with one single punch. Clearly now outnumbered, his mate acted on my suggestion that they should both empty their pockets. The other lad promptly pulled a knife on me, which he soon discovered was not the best idea he had ever had. I pocketed a large wedge of cash which I found in the lad's pocket and which more than paid for my car window. Soon the knife-wielding assailant and his semi-conscious colleague were trying to find a way out of a huge briar bush that Throbber and I had thrown them both into. This dense area of scrub would hopefully have covered them both in cuts and scratches, as they attempted to extricate themselves. We drove away quite quickly.

In 2001 I was named Top Comedy Performer in the Midlands Club Federation Clubland awards and I went along to the big night at the Pioneer club in Stoke-on-Trent. I could have driven home from the Potteries to Yorkshire at night in a couple of hours, but I instead holed up in a hotel and found myself ridiculously drunk and completely alone. A late-night phone call to my friend Tony Wayne got me through the night.

I was selected that year to appear in the prestigious Blackpool Clubland Command show, which is staged annually at the Horseshoe Bar at Blackpool Pleasure Beach, to coincide with the annual Club and Institute Union conference. I regarded going on the road as respite from the sense of dread that I felt at home. I knew at some stage I would discover exactly why I was short of money all the time, but I travelled all over the UK, performing my impression of an ostrich, constantly looking for sand.

A trip to Ayrshire in Scotland proved to be a real challenge in terms of hiding my depression. A holiday centre company had paid for my accommodation and, when not out on public show, I was holed up in my room guzzling whisky almost to oblivion.

The Northern Startrail Grand Final was a huge success again and the aforementioned singer Julie Reed Asquith scooped the £1000 first prize, plus other prize goodies.

The scene was now set for the biggest upheaval of my life thus far. I just didn't spot the signs.

*

31

A holiday in October of 2000 in Florida was when I knew for sure my marriage to Melanie would shortly be over. Looking back, I believe that both of us were ready to face our demons, but I also knew that my relationship with my children would be damaged irreparably. Around this time in my life, my assessment of my future relationship with my children was about the only thing I got right.

Christmas came and went and early in the New Year I was booked on shows featuring the Bachelors and Des O'Connor. Con and Dec Cluskey of the Bachelors sold more records during several of the Swinging 60s years then even the Beatles. They still play together today, as does their former bandmate John Stokes, who formed his own Bachelors show, and by coincidence I worked in shows with both sets of Bachelors during the same week. As for Des O'Connor, I was so looking forward to meeting him at the event we were both appearing in, at a cabaret venue in Birmingham. In the event Des breezed past me and straight onstage. Unfortunately, I didn't even get to meet him!

Taking the kids to dentists and attending school parents' evenings and the like required huge acting skills. I was a public figure in my own area and simply could not let my clenched mask of happiness slip. I think we both knew that the marriage was all but over, after 21 years. I ended the marriage in March of 2001, after forming a relationship with a singer, much younger than me, and that was the biggest mistake of my life. I beat myself up for years for such a classic and very personal error.

To my daughter I had been the first man in her life, her hero and confidante. I loved her so much and still do today. I even used to picture her face in my mind's eye at times of acute stress. My son sided with his mother and chose to stay with her. I am so proud of my son. He does most things just right to this day and maintains a good relationship with both his parents. I am now estranged from my daughter, but I have three grandchildren, two from my daughter and one from my son's marriage.

I take all the blame. I was in the words of Melanie, "a great dad but a terrible husband".

Melanie must have become so unhappy and insecure with me and because of how I functioned as a human being reflected on her life, it seemed to drive her further and further down a spiral of understandable disillusionment. Her response for many years must have driven and determined her financial decisions and I really can say no more about where all the money went. I honestly do not know to this day!

Things came to a head when I travelled by train to Camber Sands on the South Coast on business for *The Stage*. I passed through London, connecting through the London Underground with the second train. Standing on a crowded platform, a group of seven youths headed down the platform robbing people of money, mobile phones, brief cases and other stuff. I was carrying a company laptop supplied to me by the newspaper. It wasn't mine to give away, so when one of the young robbers made a grab for the case, I resisted. In fact I caught him square in the crotch with a kick which I hadn't used for years. Some of the others joined in with the attack and knives were produced. I took quite a beating, fending them off with one hand, my other hand holding on to the case for dear life. I did manage to do a little damage to two of my assailants and the cavalry arrived in the shape of what turned out to be British Transport Policemen. I was taken and given some medical attention for cuts and bruises and a slight knife wound to my fore-arm. Two of the seven were arrested at the scene due to CCTV evidence. I gave a statement and later I was informed by letter that all seven had subsequently been arrested and charged.

In Camber Sands I was reviewing an entertainment showcase and due to my violent diversion in London, I was late for the show, plus of course being battered and bruised. I stopped at a cash machine and tried to obtain a little money for general expenses. My overdraft facility was over its limit and the machine would not give me anything. I borrowed money from someone I knew in Camber Sands. To avoid embarrassment I lied, claiming that I had lost my wallet. I spent a long night in a holiday centre caravan, before returning to Yorkshire the follow-ing day, nursing my injuries and feeling desperately depressed.

I was making a real mess of things on the live/work front. I had a very public meltdown at the Showcall

Showcase in Blackpool and I was never asked to act as compere at the event again. Just three years later the Showcall Showcase was cancelled permanently.

The gigs were plentiful as ever, but I was working terribly. I could not switch off and forget the dark feelings of regret, as for some reason I decided to move in with the aforementioned young girl singer. At the age of 43, I realised that a certain old adage applied to me totally at that time: 'There's no fool like an old fool!' The relationship did not last and a year later I got out of it. Bad decisions were superseded by even worse decisions and for that I can offer no excuse, other than a mental illness which would remain undiagnosed for a further 14 years and for which I also discovered had affected my relationships for most of my life.

It was March 31st 2001 when I was booked to appear at a social club near Blackburn, Lancashire. I will never forget the club's name. It was Intack and Knuzden club, but I can't remember anything about the show itself.

I had managed to acquire some sleeping tablets and I called at an off-licence to buy a bottle of whisky. My intention was to drive through the night to the East Coast and the small picturesque coastal village of Runswick Bay, which is just north of Whitby. My intention was to end my life there during the night by swallowing a sufficient quantity of tablets and alcohol and simply walking into the sea. I had heard that freezing to death was quite a pleasurable way to die and I had just had enough.

Sometimes in life inexplicably weird things just happen. My friend Tony Wayne rang me while I was driving. I wasn't going to answer at first, but eventually I spoke to Tony, who opened the conversation with: "I think you need to talk to me, don't you?" After a long and emotional ramble down memory lane, Tony persuaded me that better times were possible and that my predicament wasn't all my fault.

Interesting assignments still came in, and that year I travelled to Belfast where I attended the Irish Arts Awards dinner and chum-up with the presenter Patrick Keilty. I worked with magician Paul Daniels in a theatre in the town of Whitehaven, Cumbria. I judged a national talent final alongside a singer called Lolly, who was in the charts at the time, and Nick Thomas, who is head of the production company Qdos.

The *Manchester Evening News* staged a talent competition final at the Willows cabaret club in Salford that year. Also, on the judging panel was the successful agent Malcolm Feld. There was also a curious character who claimed some kind of association with Robbie Williams. The owner of the Willows venue was a lovely man called John Wilkinson and it was only thanks to him that the members of the judging panel escaped unscathed after the result was announced. The huge crowd in the audience were partisan and hostile, with only the eventual winner's supporters cheering and clapping us judges. We were accompanied out to our cars by a large array of hefty muscle men/minders and we all took off out of the car park like Formula One drivers off the starting grid.

My beloved daughter Michelle took her exams and was a straight-A student. My son's scholastic achievements were not as high as his sister but I was equally proud of him. He has grown into a much better man than I could ever be. His nature is steady, solid and his view of the world is balanced and fair. I struggle to find any way at all that we are alike. Perhaps that is a good thing.

The legal wheels had begun to turn in my divorce and I was pleased to hear that Melanie had formed a new relationship.

I took my daughter and son to Spain for a week's holiday, but my misuse of alcohol ensured that I felt even worse about myself in their company. I had become an embarrassment to them and they were both old enough to know what kind of bitter, depressed and angry man their Dad had become.

We came back from Spain and I was straight back into work, speaking at a dinner at St Helens rugby league club. The other speaker was a young man who, I was informed, was a protegé of the great Ken Dodd and he was first up to speak. His material was squeaky clean and witty, but he left the rugby people in the hall pretty unmoved.

The feeling of not getting laughs from the comedian's point of view simply cannot be explained. Time seems to stand still, the spirit sinks and finding a way out of the downward spiral which the performer feels seems impossible. There are tricks we learn to dig ourselves out of trouble, but almost invariably there is no way back for a comedian if there is no significant audience reaction within the first few minutes. The young man sat down looking deflated, turned to me and said: "Your turn now, pal." I got up on my hindlegs and tore into the crowd, with every sexist and smutty gag I could think of. The lads loved the filth I was delivering, but towards the end of my spot, I glanced at a smoked glass window at the back of the room, I saw something which threw me off course and completely out of my comedy kilter, if only for a few seconds. The face of Ken Dodd was looking right back at me.

After the show, I walked out of the gents' toilet to find Ken and his young protegé deep in conversation in an alcove close to the exit. Ken waved me over and after a few initial greetings, he then gave me a bit of a lecture on the type of material I was doing. I remained respectfully silent and nodded assent to his assessment of my spot. All the time I was thinking I would rather do the rude stuff than suffer the indignity of dying the death his protegé had just suffered.

With so much going on, I was beginning to wonder how far 'down in the dumps' life could make me become. I needn't have worried for too long, as a small person from Huddersfield, who I had already known for some considerable time already, was about to reappear in my life.

My lifesaver, my best friend and later to become my wife and saviour. My Bevvy.

*

32

For many months I was living through a kind of limbo period, doing up and decorating the family home in preparation for sale. Melanie had moved into a rented house nearby and that was that.

Prior to the smoking ban in pubs and clubs, things were very different in terms of a working environment for club entertainers. I had struggled with chest problems for years and, aside from the odd cigar, I had not smoked since my days down the pit, which presented its own set of breathing hazards of course. I was invited onto BBC Radio in the spring of 2002, when moves towards a national smoking ban were being orchestrated by the widow of the entertainer Roy Castle. Roy had died back in 1994, his wife claiming that secondary smoke was the main reason for his succumbing to lung cancer. Fiona Castle and I chatted on air to a presenter about our mutual desire to see smoking end in the clubs forever. This interview made me a few more enemies amongst the smoking fraternity in the very clubs where I was booked to entertain. Perhaps this was not my wisest move and certainly demonstrated the pitfalls of being both an entertainer and a journalist.

A very strange night was had early that year in Clydach near Swansea in South Wales. I had travelled down there after an invitation from a lovely man called Bill O'Callaghan to attend and review a trade showcase of talented Welsh acts. In charge of the technical side of things was a man I used to work with at Showcall Showcase in Blackpool who, as I alluded to earlier, had apparently caught my young singing lady ex on the rebound. At that time their relationship was something they were both being rather circumspect about. I have no idea why. I didn't care. I wished this lady nothing but happiness and was sorry to hear their relationship had ended in divorce, very quickly after they married. His name is John. He clearly did not know that I was already well aware of his new girlfriend, but he seemed to want the whole thing to remain a secret, so I played along and said nothing.

In 2002 I broke a big story for *The Stage* concerning certain financial regulations which entertainment agents were going to have to comply with going forward. There had been many convictions of rogue agents misappropriating fees and monies which should have been passed on to artistes and acts they represented. The new regulation meant that the agent's money would effectively be separated at source from the artistes and acts. I certainly made one or two powerful enemies that day too, as I had been very active behind the scenes in making this legislation come about in the first place.

In 2002 I started to give a helping hand to a young singer and musician from Leeds. His name was Peter Grant and, after introducing him to the right people, young Peter ended up with a Top Ten album and a short spell of true fame. Peter changed direction musically for his second album and the record company just threw him off the gravy train when sales did not materialise. The last I heard of young Peter, he was living in Spain and musically I'm not sure what he is up to. I hope Peter finds his way back into the spotlight again, if that is what he wishes for.

The family home was up on the market and subsequently sold very quickly indeed to a couple with a young family, which was one less thing to worry about.

Things were becoming increasingly strained at *The Stage*, with a meeting on September 5th 2002 in London which saw me lose my cool. The frustration of working for people who were happy to take such a huge amount of their advertising revenue from the sector they dismissively dubbed 'Light Ents' but were reluctant to provide any notable news coverage of the scene left me baffled and confused. My diary records at that time indicate that I didn't want to push too hard as they were sending me good money every month and in the land of the self-employed, we do not bite the hand that feeds.

A short theatre tour put me on the same bill as Irish comedian Frank Carson in the late summer of 2002. Some of the venues we visited, such as one rather grand place in Chester, were more accustomed to hosting actors then entertainers. There really was a condescending and snide side to some of the highbrow theatre staff when we mere mortals, who they described as 'variety turns', found our way down into the hallowed corridors normally occupied solely by our thespian friends.

The year ended with a New Year's Eve booking at the

Barnbow club in Leeds. The club was originally built for the staff of the military tank and armaments factory. Given the fact that I felt as though 2002 had been just another year of conflict, the venue seemed somehow apt.

*

33

On February of 2003 I bought a house, much smaller than the family home, but 32 Beckbridge Way, Normanton came along at just the right time. My son could come to the house and eat after school before being picked up by his mum, as my new home was just few-minutes away from his school. My daughter chose to live with me and for a while, things settled down a little.

My daughter had been accepted at New College, Pontefract, proving yet again that she seemed able to switch off all other thoughts and worries and focus on her studies. Today she is now a social worker and though I never see her, I am very proud of her achievements.

By May 2003 Bevvy and me were an item, but we were taking things very slowly indeed. Neither of us wanted to learn from any more of life's harsh lessons.

Nice work still seemed to be coming my way, despite the fact that I didn't feel focused or able to concentrate on being a stage performer any more.

I was booked on a trip to the Isle of Man, where I was asked to act as compere for the re-opening of the Villa Marina Hall, on the seafront in Douglas. The place is a gem in the collection of the 28 or so buildings in the UK which remain that were built by Victorian architect Frank Matcham. Elkie Brooks and her band and the comedian Tom O'Connor were amongst an all-star cast on the bill.

The flight was late due to an oil spillage on the runway

at Ronaldsway airport and I finally arrived quite stressed at my hotel. I walked into the venue and was introduced to Seamus Heaney, the show producer. I was shown to my dressing room, which was way too hot but was right next door to the green room. For the uninitiated, a green room in a theatre is where food, drinks and all manner of hospitality is made available to the artistes and stage crew. Through a crack in the door jamb I could see Tom O'Connor speaking to a man seated in a winged leather chair.

Before I conclude this anecdote, I should perhaps mention that at this time, I believed there to be only four true British-born comedy genius figures ever: Charlie Chaplin, Stan Laurel, Tony Hancock and Norman Wisdom. Norman was by then SIR Norman Wisdom and I knew that he lived on the island. I do not generally indulge in hero worship but, with my only living comedy hero sitting right in front of me, I was genuinely and noticeably in awe, as Norman sprang out of his chair to attention, in true comic style, right in front of me and introduced himself. The diminutive Norman was comedy royalty and this was the biggest *wow!* moment of my show business life.

The show went well but I was tired and didn't attend the after-show party. Breakfast with Tom O'Connor the following morning was a pleasure. Tom was once a big star on television and he proved to be amusing and absorbing company.

In the March of 2002, I had started booking all the cabarets and helping select entertainment staff for

Thornwick Bay and Sea Farm holiday centre in East Yorkshire, then the largest independently owned park of its kind in the UK. Ian Sandy and I were becoming very close. He introduced me to a man called Dan Chen, who he claimed was a work colleague at his company and introduced Dan as "my number two". Ian and I were close right through to his death in 2012. In the same year, I also began to cover the regular adults-only room compere's night off and put shows on every Tuesday at this venue on the Yorkshire coast throughout the summer season.

More telly followed when Yorkshire television producer Jane Hickson booked me a documentary called *The Magic of Clubland*, which was presented by a very good and talented man called Ian Clayton.

I was always a fan of the Perry & Croft penned sit-com *'Allo 'Allo*. The actress Sue Hodge played the part of the diminutive waitress Mimi Le Bonk and I was delighted when I was given the job of reviewing a show featuring Sue at the Bonnington theatre in Arnold, Nottinghamshire. The show was called *Mimi and the Boy* and this was basically Sue in character as Mimi accompanied by a pianist, the eponymous 'Boy'. Sue regaled her audience with stories from the hit show and other comedy vehicles she has been involved in. The producer Tony Sherwood, such a delightful man, took me backstage to meet the lovely Sue. The show was a success and we remain friends to this day.

Louise Grainger of the actors and entertainer's union Equity, had organised a variety workshop that year, along with the singing star Barb Jungr. I was asked to go along to a small cabaret venue in Soho and present the show. This was mainly actors trying to learn new skills. Ms Grainger is a very good friend and those present seemed to know quite a lot about me. A woman performer seemed rather preoccupied with asking me about how I have survived so long on Northern Clubland stages. She asked me if all the stories were true, expecting me perhaps to claim that exaggeration was a factor within the tales of bingo, baying mobs and booing crowds. I assured this lady and others who seemed to be hanging on my every word that absolutely everything they had heard were probably true and all the stories were only the tip of the iceberg.

The final question I was asked by this very nice actor lady shook me a little. She enquired: "Doesn't all that pressure damage you as an artiste and a person?" I simply replied in the affirmative, adding: "And I am living proof of the fact."

During that London visit I had another superstar close encounter. Sting walked casually over to me. I was wearing an ID badge, which was the only reason he knew who I was. He stuck out his hand and said: "Hi Mark, I think you're expecting me!" I was told later that Sting had eschewed the option of a chauffeur-driven ride around from the Connaught Hotel where he was staying. He happened to be in town and his role at the function was to support the Musicians Union and Equity by making a personal appearance. He and his pal/minder strolled around from Mayfair into Soho, where we met inside the venue.

I love his music and I was always a fan of his first band, the Police. I also know that he used to work as a pit-musician in an orchestra and as a cabaret backing musician, so we are probably cut from the same cloth. It all went swimmingly, but as I was then and remain an overweight and unappealing Northern singer and comic, I found that for the sake of my already fragile ego, I didn't want to stand right next to Sting, aka Gordon Sumner, for very long.

I was still covering trade showcase events for *The Stage*, and a trip to Camberley in Surrey was extremely entertaining. The owner of the Lakeside complex at Camberley is Bob Potter. A friend of royalty and a successful businessman, Bob still worked hard despite the fact that, at that time, he had recently become an octogenarian. Bob gave me a lovely room in one of his hotels and took me on a guided tour around the many acres of his impressive gaffe.

Bob was about to open a new golf course, but a series of night-time raids from burglars had stymied the progress on construction. The bad guys were accessing the land by ram-raiding a rather fragile-looking wooden gate, which Bob had kept paying to be mended.

During the night of my visit, the intruders had ram-raided the gate again only to discover that Bob had arranged a surprise for them. A huge pit had been dug the day before and, using the same modus operandi as before by smashing through the gate, the criminal gang sunk into the very deep pit, wedging them all tightly into the cab of the vehicle. Local police turned up shortly after to complete the formalities.

It was 2.30am when Bob Potter and I sat in his billiard room within his lovely home, close to the club and complex which he himself created. We sat enjoying a lovely single malt whisky and Bob showed me his vast collection of show business memorabilia. Eventually I pleaded exhaustion, adding that I had to catch an early train back into London. Bob looked as fresh as a daisy and I was even more surprised to see him grazing his way along a breakfast buffet in the hotel just four hours after we had parted.

The night before a couple of illuminated letters had gone dark on his hotel sign. Whilst passing in his car around midnight, Bob picked up his phone and rang someone. "Will they answer at this time of night?" I enquired. Bob's reply was: "Oh! Yes. I'm a very good customer." Whilst toying casually and sleepily with toast and coffee at breakfast, I glanced outside and beheld the spectacle of two men climbing up the ladders and bringing the sign letters back to life. Bob dropped me off at Aldershot railway station a little later. He said goodbye with a cheery: "Be lucky!" Show business royalty? Oh yes. Absolutely!

By then my roadie Throbber and his partner Jane had moved to live on the island of Cyprus and in June 2003 I went to visit them. Their new home was in a small inland village close to the town of Paralimni. They were living in a two-bedroom apartment right next to the border checkpoint between the Greek and Turkish sides.

A car journey on a road very close to the border was scary, with Turkish Cypriots training their rifles on us from their watch towers. I asked Throbber what would happen if we broke down or got a puncture? Throbber replied that one of the many white UN helicopters, which circled over our heads at regular intervals, would no doubt come to our rescue. The lady who owned the apartment building where Throbber lived had a great vantage point on the roof of the building, where strong telescopes and binoculars could be borrowed in order to gaze into the so-called ghost resort of Famagusta, which is on the Turkish side. Things have changed now in terms of the ease of crossings between the Greek and Turkish sides, but the balloon could still go up at any time, especially with Syria just a few sea miles away.

An avuncular and worldly-wise agent and promoter called Les Bather rang to ask me if I would like to join the second tour of the *Laughter – My Arse!* show with Ricky Tomlinson. This time around the show cast would comprise Ricky of course, plus actor and comedian Michael Starke, Nat King Cole tribute singer Bernie Wenton, comedian Eddie Archer, impressionist Stevie Riks and myself. I found out at the eleventh hour that they needed a great female singer to complete the ensemble. Les had also booked the singer, who up to only recently I had been in a relationship with. The tour was awkward to say the very least.

It was time for me to sign off as compere of the talent show *Northern Startrail* and I handed over to my former assistant Danny Andrews. Danny put a new team together, moved the whole event to a working men's club in Sheffield – and two seasons later the whole project sank without trace.

At Christmas my son and daughter went to their Mum's house and, although my Bevvy had invited me to her place, I decided to remain quite alone at home. By now Bevvy was my only hope. My mind was all over the place and my GP was doling out the happy pills.

*

34

I managed to renew my acquaintance albeit briefly with Jane McDonald who had turned up in the audience at a benefit show where I was appearing as compere. The show was aiding a poorly showbusiness friend and I had always tried to help friends in need at that time. Years later I was to find a distinct lack of reciprocity towards me when I needed help myself. It is hard not to sound bitter or resentful, but I am and try as I might, I have never been able to shut out the feelings in my mind.

Jane McDonald was appearing at the time as a regular panellist in the ITV daytime show *Loose Women*. She has been busy and famous since and is now even a BAFTA winner, which is pretty fantastic for a lass from Wakefield.

I heard that the show business legend that was Jimmy Corrigan had recently died. I found my memory going back a decade before, when Corrigan was trying to open up a new variety club close to the site of the old Wakefield Theatre club. I met him at that time and he was keen to cultivate my friendship and support due to my local newspaper columns and their perceived influence.

In partnership with his friend, the financier and brewery boss Dick Forbes Watson, Jimmy hoped to build a second Batley Variety club. After all, he was the man who had built the original Batley venue and booked some of the biggest stars on the planet, back in the Swinging 60s.

Corrigan once told me a story of booking Louis Armstrong and his orchestra. The orchestra flew across the Pond first, with Satchmo following the day after. Corrigan had his superstar guest staying at his own mansion. On the day of his arrival in what was then an unprepossessing Yorkshire mill town, Corrigan picked Armstrong up in his Rolls-Royce and stopped outside an old scout hut, with a fragile wooden sign 'Batley Variety Club' swinging from the front door. Once inside Armstrong walked into a dusty, room filled with rickety tables, which were covered in ashtrays and dirty table cloths. It took a while for the penny to drop and once Mr Armstrong started laughing, he couldn't stop. It was of course a huge practical joke. The pair then returned to the 'Roller' and finished the short journey to the real, brand spanking new variety club.

Thoughts of news on Corrigan's demise led me to remember that back in the early 90s, the club Corrigan opened in Wakefield was called 'Corrigan's' and the singer and 60s star Ronnie Hilton was booked for the opening night. As was the case with Hilton's show-business career, the days of the variety clubs had come and gone. None of the new telly stars wanted to work in such venues and the people who used to go to the original variety clubs by then all belonged to a different generation.

Corrigan's sank without trace.

During 2004 I decided to go on a health kick and I managed to lose five stones in weight. I began to struggle with my weight in my mid-30s and today, due to a multitude of health problems and injuries, I remain overweight. Back then I worked hard in the gym and felt great. How I wish my fitness fling had lasted.

In the May of 2004, I headed for Belfast on business for *The Stage*. A trip to a show being staged at the Ulster Maple Leaf club ended rather scarily. During the evening some guests from an Orange Lodge seemed to be creating tension between themselves and a group from a Catholic club association of some sort. Some British military personnel were trying to keep things jolly, but as my hotel was only a few hundred yards away at the top of the street, I decided to leave just before the end.

I was told later that a fight had broken out at the end of the evening. There had been reports on the news of cars cruising around targeting tourists and attacking them for no apparent reason. Some Australian tourists became involved in just such an attack earlier that week. A car slowed down to check me out, as I walked briskly up the road towards the safety of my hotel. Another car appeared behind and the first car sped away.

On a previous Belfast trip, I had visited a social club within Shorts aircraft factory complex. An announcement over the club PA system warned everyone not to go outside for any reason, as a sniper had been shooting at the building and the army were on their way. As an entertainment show reviewer, I never even consider there would be any necessity to apply for danger money.

In 2005 I was booked as a judge for the British Resorts

Association Talent show final, which was won by a young singer, who coincidentally lived quite close to me. I knew Chris Lafferty as his vocal technique tutor was my great friend Tony Wayne. Lafferty scooped the £2000 first prize and became involved with one or two influential London-based people, including the erudite performer and producer Kaplan Kaye. Young Lafferty subsequently appeared at a Royal Gala show at the Theatre Royal Windsor, which was attended by HRH the Duke of Edinburgh. Other stars on the bill included Engelbert Humperdinck and Joe Pasquale.

The world was at the feet of young Chris Lafferty, until his problems in keeping his hands off the property of others emerged. He also served some time in prison for passing himself off as a teacher, presenting fake documentation. All of which proved to me yet again that some people have the necessary mental attributes to attain and retain stardom and some simply don't.

Another who fits that category is Danny Tetley. Danny had reached the final of my own talent show *Northern Startrail* some years ago. In 2018 Tetley, from Bradford, shot to fame in *The X Factor*, where he almost went all the way in the final stages. Those of us who knew him also knew that Danny Tetley was a ticking timebomb. He was filmed feeding his expensive cocaine addiction, a story which reached the celebrity obsessed tabloid press and he then turned out to be a paedophile. Tetley was convicted and jailed for a number of charges concerning his involvement with very young teenage boys.

I myself was enjoying great happiness in June of 2004 as I went away on my first holiday with Bevvy. We enjoyed a great time on the Greek island of Zante and I just knew I was also in a good place mentally.

*

35

Ever-decreasing circles. That was the feeling of performing on the ever-contracting club scene during the 90s. Same circuit, but one by one the clubs continued to fall. The major industries had all but gone and the communities who used to work and play together seemed fragmented and fractured within sections of each other.

I managed however to spark Bevvy's love affair with musical theatre in 2005, as I took her along to the Alhambra Theatre in Bradford to see a touring production of *Jesus Christ Superstar*.

A charity event, which I agreed to appear in South Yorkshire didn't turn out to be quite as I expected. The event organiser, who used to be a friend of mine, had managed to attract a big crowd, due to a number of big names who had pledged to appear. The downside was that the organiser spotted a friend of hers in the audience right at the finale of the show. The person she spotted, an ex-professional singer, had only recently been released from prison and was a convicted paedophile. Bevvy had very strong and compelling reasons to stay away from such people and knowing the reasons for her feelings, which I won't go into here, I looked on in horror as the organiser coaxed the paedophile/ex-entertainer on to the stage for a late-night singalong. A very well-known comedian, who is also a pantomime legend and could ill afford to be seen in such company, promptly ducked out and simply walked off stage. I followed him and headed for the exit door. We were both very angry at the potential risk of being photographed on a stage with a known sex offender and I saw Bevvy's ashen face and knew I had to get the hell out of there.

The following day I rang the organiser to express my reasons for ducking out so quickly. Her reply was: "I know he was innocent and my children grew up in this man's company and he never harmed any of my kids." I now realise this was the beginning of the end of this friendship. This particular friend had suffered much sadness in her own life which may have impaired her judgement in certain matters. I had done my best to help this person over the years with a variety of her work and family problems. Yet again it seems that I had placed misguided trust in the untrustworthy. In 2015 I discovered this particular person had been part of a group of people who tried and succeeded in contributing to my own mounting business problems, with the motive apparently being money. During recent times this person had caught the Facebook bug and was and as far as I know still remains immersed in this platform for the self-absorbed, which has in so many cases become a substitute for aspects of the real world and a refuge from its more unpalatable realities.

In May of 2005 my daughter went out to a party that is known in school-leaver circles these days as a 'prom'. I took her out in the afternoon for her posh hair-do and bought her a gown. I was so proud of her as I drove her along to the prom to meet her friends.

My son Steven had a real aptitude for music and was doing well as a young pianist. He could also play the drums and was destined to head for music college. I couldn't have been more proud of my children than I was.

My friend, the club owner and former rugby league star David Sampson invited me to a dinner he had organised at his club one night. The after-dinner speakers were comedian Gary Skyner, who self-deprecatingly bills himself as the 'small-arms dealer from Liverpool' due to his status as one of the so-called Thalidomide babies who were born deformed, due to a drug which was taken by pregnant women at that time to combat nausea but had tragic side effects.

His fellow speaker was a genuine London gangster. 'Mad' Frankie Fraser was his name and due to the fact that I knew his biographer Patrick Newley and the cachet of being a newspaper journalist, I was introduced to Mr Fraser, who was accompanied by a genuine top-drawer minder. Contrary to popular belief, top minders (and I do recognise them when I see them) are never muscle-bound thugs, covered in tattoos and possessing no social skills. The real top men hover in the background, barely noticeable and observe absolutely everything.

Mad Frankie's crimes are well documented, but all I can say is that he was a perfect gentleman to me. The softness of his hands during our handshake told me Frankie had never done a day's work in his life, but he had tremendous presence and made eye-contact immediately, just as any man of this type would. After all, he had probably been sussing people out quickly all his life. I happen to know that many in the packed audience were off-duty policemen and during the Q&A session, they were giving Frankie a bit of a hard time with loaded questions such as "Aren't you ashamed of the crimes you committed?" etcetera.

I decided to throw Frankie a lifeline and raised my hand to ask my own question. Recognising me as a friendly face, Frankie picked me out immediately. I asked: "What are the differences between the villains back in your day, such as the Krays, the Richardsons and yourself and the villains who operate today?" Frankie's expression turned from pressure to pleasure as he reminisced that in his violent heydays people were safe to walk the streets and that villains then only hurt other villains. He added: "These days it's all about drugs. It wasn't then."

One of my favourite singers was the great American performer Alexander O'Neal and in October of 2005 I had the chance to meet the star and see him perform at Stratford arts centre. I'm not sure exactly what was wrong with Mr O'Neal on the night, but his trousers fell down onstage and he seemed not entirely focused on the job in hand. Somehow the whole experience made me feel quite depressed.

Equally depressing was the decision by *The Stage* MD Catherine Comerford to move the Showcall Showcase to the Stardust club near Leicester. I knew the venue was unsuitable, but I was never consulted. One of the last of the great variety clubs still in operation at that time, this fine club had by then seen much better days. In 2008 the venue was sold and now operates as a sort of market.

My many trips to Scotland often featured interaction with a friendly Irish agent called Glyn Davies. Glyn really knew how to look after people, and to save me taxi money he lent me his brand-new Jaguar car to drive around Edinburgh. I was shocked and saddened to hear that Glyn had been convicted of sex crimes and he went to prison as a paedophile. Who knows what is really in a person's head? Some are harder to read then others!

My great friend, the singer Michael France died in 2005. His real name was Mick Brassington and he had been lead-singer of a successful band called Method, who were managed for a while by ex-Beatle Ringo Starr. The band later changed their name to Stormer. Due to a serious injury which he sustained many years before, Mick's life was blighted by pain and the painkilling regime he was forced to follow was rigorous. He was a good man and a kind man, as well as possessing a remarkable singing voice – and that isn't a bad epitaph.

Another close friend Howard Burnette died in Spain and the outpouring of love after his death raised a lot of funds for the two children he left behind. Howard's ex-wife Angie, a Mormon, adopted the children, and a series of fundraising shows were organised, all of which I either appeared in or attended. The last was at Wakefield City club in December 2005. Howard was a one-off. A likeable rogue. A true character. An enigma. We will probably never see his like again, but he is long gone now, as is the Wakefield City club, which is built over these days and only a memory.

*

36

I have always been fond of a man called David Hill, who runs a management agency and is an actor, pantomime Dame and all-round good guy. I spent some time on business with David on the island of Majorca some years ago, which was particularly memorable.

Another evening spent with David in his native Brighton provided quite a shock to the system. David's great friend was the late, great comedy actress Dora Bryan and this much-loved lady attended a show David had produced in a cabaret room near Hove.

Dora was accompanied by her little dog and I was writing a review of the event, which was being presented by the brilliant comedian Paul Eastwood, who in my view really should be a massive comedy star by now. Tables and chairs were set out cabaret style and Dora seated herself directly opposite me. The lights went down and Mr Eastwood walked out onstage. I should add that, at this stage, I had not even noticed this tiny pooch, until out of the darkness Dora's canine pal appeared suddenly by putting his head over the screen of my laptop. I almost jumped out of my skin and, much to the amusement of everyone present, I fell off my seat in shock.

It is fair to say that Dora liked a drink and she was laughing so much she spilt her vodka all over the place. Chaos reigned for a while and David was laughing so much that he was bent double in paroxysms of mirth.

Dora Bryan, who I used to love to watch on television in her hit show *According to Dora* when I was a child, was a national treasure. Her last part of any note was a hilarious portrayal of a randy, wobbly old lady in Victoria Wood's celebrated sit-com *dinnerladies*. Dora died in 2014.

I was invited one day by *The Stage* editor Brian Attwood to attend a lunchtime meeting at the Savage club in London one day. The club is situated in the heart of Westminster and is for 'Bohemian gentlemen involved in the Arts'. Non-members are asked to bang a sort of Indian drum and mutter some kind of incantation before entering the bar area. Spending the day there with all these 'Bohemians' was an eye-opener. I honestly thought for a moment I had travelled backwards in time and that Bertie Wooster and his chums were about drag PG Wodehouse in and engage him to write more stories on the subject of British eccentricity.

A holiday in Bulgaria in 2007 was comparable to spending time in Venice. There were huge electric storms and the place was completely flooded out. The morning after the main storm, there was no electric and I went out onto the main promenade in the resort in search of food and drink, as our hotel was offering next to nothing. I almost got more than I bargained for! I waded down a street and spotted a bar, which was illuminated by gaslights. The owner was at the door and he beckoned me over. He then made me quite an offer. He said: "Okay sir, I speak English. We cook with gas here so I can do you a great price for a steak meal and wine." The man then pointed upwards where I beheld the vision of a half a dozen or so semi-naked ladies. The man continued: "You can go upstairs and have the girl of your choice before or after you eat. It's all in with the price." I returned to the hotel and told Bevvy, who for some reason thought the whole story was hysterically funny. I'm not sure the concept of sex with every steak meal will ever catch on here in the UK

Tony Peers is a comedian, show producer, actor, pantomime Dame and one of the finest show business fellows I have ever known. At that time Tony was booking me into a chain of hotel venues, which all presented full cabaret floor shows in the resorts of Folkestone, Llandudno, Blackpool and Scarborough. I worked them all for many years and enjoyed some great nights. One night at the Metropole in Blackpool a lone old gentleman seated right at the front actually fell asleep while I was telling gags. Snoring loudly, the man was getting many more laughs then I was, before suddenly waking up and realising what was going on. Much to the amusement of the audience, the man arose from his slumber and received a round of sarcastic applause as he shuffled off to bed.

I spent much of Christmas 2007 in cabaret at the Grand Hotel Scarborough. The beautiful ballroom there even boasts a theatre circle. There were backing musicians, resident dancers and singers and a compere. When Tony lost the contract to another company, much of the show specifications were downgraded. There were also new owners, who clearly realised the cost of everything and the value of nothing. So sad.

In 2007/08 I appeared in pantomime for the first time in my career. I was cast as Ugly Sister in Tony Peers Productions' version of *Cinderella*. The venue was the Parr Hall theatre in Warrington and I was well outside my comfort zone.

Actors have a much different methodology to the job in hand to entertainers and I think it is fair to say that the director didn't rate me much. Working for *The Stage*, I wrote a lovely full feature about my experiences and the reaction I received once it was published was a delight and lifted my morale no end.

The show attracted favourable reviews, but I found the whole thing quite a stretch, especially on days when there were three performances. A school's performance at 11am was followed by a matinee at 2.30pm and then there was also an evening performance at 7pm. Sitting in the wings, with my heavy, cumbersome costume and full make-up on, I looked through a slit in the tabs and noticed my great friend Tony Wayne seated right on the front row. Tony was running his stage school at that time and had hired a 52-seater coach, which he filled with staff and students, who filled the front rows of the stalls. My Ugly Sister partner was an actor called Ian Ganderton and we entered from opposite sides of the stage. All I could hear was Tony's infectious and extremely loud laugh as he witnessed my debut as a professional transvestite.

*

—37—

In 2008 I started working regularly in cabaret for a well-known casino company. The audiences were not always too engaged, but at least the work paid well. Between March and October my onstage work life consisted mainly of performing as resident compere at Thornwick Bay and Sea Farm holiday centre and sick of schlepping around the ever-contracting club circuit, the holiday centre became my focus.

Before I arrived to commence my duties at Thornwick Bay, in the adults-only cabaret room known as the Coble Bar, the lunatics had clearly taken over the asylum. Many regular visitors within the room seemingly laboured under the misapprehension that they themselves were actually running the place. The regulars were caravan owners. Some of them stayed on the site for the entire eight-month duration the place was open annually. Others came every weekend, while a minority were more occasional visitors. During the high summer the holiday-makers came and went, with many renting caravans and chalets.

None of my predecessors had perfected the trick of bringing everyone together. Instead the folks sat in their same seats every week, apparently in the belief the seats had been reserved especially for them. I had seven and a half successful seasons in the job. The site owners and Ian Sandy himself, who had hired me to do the job, were not optimistic that the warring and bickering factions within the room could be brought together and this was indeed a very strange room when I set up to make a success of it.

Bevvy came in with me and I soon nicknamed her 'Bingo Bev', as she began the bingo-calling duties. Bevvy proved to be a great stooge and she derived her own methods of getting a laugh. During the onstage banter between us, I simply let her have the last laugh, which of course produced the biggest laugh of all.

Over the next few years, we assembled a cast straight out of the audience, who took part in sketches and I wrote and produced three adult pantomimes, which the regulars took part in enthusiastically. The ThornWick Amateur Theatrical Society, bearing the acronym 'TWATS', was born and our shows included *Cinderella Finds Her Dick, Nobbin' Hood and the Sexy Babes in the Wood* and *Snow White and the Seven Giants*. There was poetry corner with a lady who dubbed herself the 'Sexy Chantelle' and I gave people specific tasks such as dressing men up as 'dolly dealers' for a regular *Play Your Cards Right* gameshow. Others became involved by writing comedy scripts of their own to be read out in front of the audience just to see who got the biggest laughs from the audience. There was also some tip-top cabaret acts and all manner of comedy shenanigans. The cabaret room became successful, when before it was considered more than once to close the place and concentrate on the family cabaret venue next door.

All was set fair and for a long time all was well. I

learned long ago that entertainers will never be able to please everyone and there still were a few dissenting voices. There was a gang of barflies who only used to come in towards the end of the evening. They displayed a huge sense of entitlement and an exaggerated sense of their own collective importance. You can't win them all, so I just didn't engage with them more than I had to. Amongst the remaining dissenting voices was a character who everyone knew as 'Gino'. He fancied himself as a singer, but he was a sulky and childish individual who managed to cause the occasional bit of friction for reasons best known to himself.

In charge of the family entertainment in the other cabaret room was a young man with a very high opinion of himself. I had him sussed in five minutes flat and later I was proved to be bang on the money. This young man worked for Ian Sandy on another project at the Snowdome venue in Tamworth Staffordshire during the winter. When Ian came under a little pressure from the owners there, this chap went behind Ian's back and tried to obtain the entertainment contract himself. He failed. As you will read further on, he played exactly the same tactic when I came under pressure at Thornwick. He failed then too, but for entirely different reasons.

Meanwhile in London at *The Stage*, the MD Catherine Comerford had purchased a piece of expensive computer software. Entertainment agents protect their interests very carefully and the software was intended to provide an opportunity for entertainment bookers to source live entertainers. Although the piece of software was intended to be 'agent friendly', it seems Ms Comerford's advisers simply did not seem to comprehend the way our business works. Intended as a new income stream, the product was doomed to failure from the start. I was consulted but only after the scheme was launched and my reply was to point out the sheer folly of the scheme. My reply was truthful and succinct and Ms Comerford shot the messenger. Perhaps I am overstating a little here, but there is no doubt in my mind that this was the exact juncture when I began to be sidelined and marginalised by people I had tried so hard to help and promote.

On a brighter note, I produced another huge charity cabaret event in 2008 called *Clubland Live – Like It Used to Be*. Without a backing track in sight, a brilliant live band led by musical director Terry Bell provided accompaniment for myself and my huge cast of great singers. The cast comprised the proud owners of some of the best of Clubland voices, including Lisa Pearson, Tony Wayne, Johnnie Martell, Karen King, Laura Ellis, Siobhan Phillips, Jade Adams, Paul Stewart and many others. A lovely man called Kevin Berry was working at *The Stage* by then and he came along to review the show. Not too long after this, Kevin asked me to help with the entertainment at his dual retirement and birthday party, which was staged within his lovely home in the old North Yorkshire Quaker village of Aireton. Kevin was a fine human being. Kevin's wife Pat was a delight and Kevin's ever faithful dog Bryn was a welcome guest joining the mourners at Kevin's funeral in 2013.

On the home front, I had money in the bank from the

sale of Beckbridge Way. My daughter had moved in with her boyfriend and had eschewed the option of going to university and instead went out into the world of work. My son continued to live with his mum and her new husband, and I just wasn't sure what to do next.

Bevvy and I decided we would rent somewhere for a year or two and weigh up our options over a period of time. We moved into a spacious house in an area called Horse Race End near Wakefield. The neighbours were related to our landlords and were a man and wife team, who were both barking mad. I am not and have never been a patient man and perhaps the least said about this pair the better. Suffice it to say, that no one wanted to stay in the house very long, and tenants came and went very frequently. We stayed there for a while before escaping to live in the nearby peaceful village of Kirkthorpe. I was very happy in my new home from the off and I now have a place which I hope to stay in until my dying day. Our village is tiny and our home life is now settled and happy.

On the journalistic front, I travelled to Blackpool one day and visited the home of the legend that was Duggie Chapman. Duggie was a variety entertainer who started a successful career as a show producer. He was behind a million seaside shows during the glory years of summer season and variety. His wife was Beryl Johnson, a singer whose voice Duggie waxed lyrically about, comparing his beloved Beryl's dulcet tones as "like a lark ascending".

I went along to see one of Duggie's shows at the Lowther Pavilions in Lytham St Annes and on another evening, I went to see his production that summer within the Winter Gardens Blackpool. The shows were mainly wartime theme shows and Old Time Music Hall type productions. The audiences were mainly elderly, and on-stage the shows featured performers such as camp comedy piano star Mike Terry, trombone man Pete Lindup, and magician and pickpocket Mark Raffles.

In 2009 Duggie pulled off a huge coup by signing Michael Barrymore up for a series of Saturday evening shows on the North Pier in Blackpool. Duggie spent a small fortune in promotion and advertising, but those aggrieved about the death of Stuart Lubbock, who was discovered dead in Barrymore's swimming pool at his home in Surrey back in 2001, made their voices heard and Barrymore pulled out of the shows at the eleventh hour, citing an injury sustained whilst horse-riding as the reason for his withdrawal.

I met and chatted with Barrymore once or twice down the years. He always struck me as a major talent, who had reached the summit in his career and, like so many others who have attained the same status, he then looked down in horror only to discover that he was in fact afraid of these heights and didn't care for the view.

My son was performing gigs as a member of a new indie rock band called Ladderdance and I went along to Wakefield college, where he was studying music. I was one proud Dad as Steven and his bandmates clambered onstage and played their set.

Many years before my first wife and I used to enjoy holidays in and around the resort of Fuengerola on Spain's Costa Del Sol. I took Bevvy there for her first visit to the area in 2008. We caught the train from Malaga airport and got off at the stop in the suburb of Los Boliches. Our hotel was bang on the seafront and we were informed on arrival that we had been ungraded free and would now be occupying the penthouse suite no less.

Pleased but puzzled at our VIP status, it soon become clear regarding what was the true reason for our unexpected preferential treatment. It turned out to be more about logistics and practicality, as we were the only able-bodied guests in the building and moving around the hotel or attempting to access the breakfast room really was far from easy. A coachload of blind guests was rapidly followed at the check-in by a coachload of wheelchair-users. The day after another coach arrived. This final coach appeared to contain profoundly mentally disabled adults and their helpers. The place was ram-jam full of wheelchairs, walking frames, guide dogs and specialist mobility equipment. It seems the hotel management figured that keeping us ensconced in the penthouse suite would at least ensure that we did not spend quite so long in the public areas of the hotel, amongst people less fortunate than ourselves. With the breakfast buffet largely unnavigable due to the plethora of wheelchairs and walking frames, Bevvy and I decided that eating out was by far the easiest option.

In the autumn of 2008, I attended the Entertainment Agents' Association annual charity show. This was the start of a rather unnerving episode in my life. Entertainers are a strange breed. You can stand in front of some, look straight into their eyes and tell them that, in your opinion, they are absolutely brilliant onstage, or that they possess zero talent and should get as far away from show business as possible, as quickly as they can. The majority wouldn't bat an eyelid either way.

There are however a large minority of entertainers who someone could mention 99 favourable aspects about their talents and one unfavourable aspect and the entertainer would fixate solely on the one thing they didn't want to hear.

Therefore, life as a show reviewer/critic can be fraught with the unrequited attentions of the boot-lickers and back-stabbers. I manage to spot most and, Kipling-like, I 'treat those two imposters just the same'. The agents' show was staged at a club in Aspull, Lancashire and, aside from a little nastiness from the compere, a great singer with a double-barrelled name and a large chip on his shoulder, the evening passed off quite well. Once the reviews appeared, I began to receive anonymous phone calls, death threats and poison pen letters, which were sent to my home address. The data protection act determines that professional business people cannot and should not give out personal contact details, but somehow someone had obtained my address. The point of sending the threats to my home was clearly an attempt to intimidate me.

I thought that reporting the matter to the police was a priority, especially since the writer described exactly what I was wearing at the show in Aspull, correctly identified the after-shave lotion I was wearing and also described what Bevvy, who had accompanied me on the night, was wearing and the detail of a conversation he/she claimed to have engaged in with Bevvy on the night.

About that time, there was a young woman entertainer who was, for reasons best known to herself, trying to establish a relationship with me. Knowing full well of my relationship with Bevvy, this person made the mistake in engaging in text messages with me, which I kept on my phone for future reference. Rebuffing her advances seem to make no impression on her and eventually she began to try and make trouble. I drew her out to see how far she would go and soon the threats began. I put two and two together and I think I made four. The woman who has since established herself as a destructive marriage-breaker in relation to showbusiness men she perceives to be in some way powerful or influential, had a close friend, who had been sitting close to me that night in Aspull. It didn't take Sherlock Holmes to crack this case.

On a happier note, in the November of 2008, Bevvy and I flew out to Australia to stay at the home of my great friends Baz and Sue Smith, who used to work on the band scene in the Yorkshire clubs with me many moons ago. Their lovely home is in a place called Windaroo near Brisbane and is quite picturesque. We took the flight which goes via Dubai and Singapore and we even took an internal flight down to Sydney and spent a few days in a hotel there. Unfortunately, neither Bevvy nor I were very well at the time, and if we ever make that journey again to the land down under, we would certainly do things very differently.

Bevvy got to live her dream by visiting the Steve Irwin

zoo in northern Queensland and I took the opportunity to visit Toowong cemetery in the suburb of Ipswich in Brisbane, to stand at the grave of one of the three men I believe I have irrefutably proved to be involved in the so-called Whitechapel murders of 1888. The whole Jack the Ripper thing has fascinated me almost all my life.

*

38

A holiday in the Egyptian resort of Sharm el-Sheikh resulted in Bevvy and I becoming engaged to be married. I ushered Bevvy into Hassan's jewellers and I soon realised that my life had turned right around and there was so much positivity and optimism. As the children's song goes, I was happy and I knew it, so I clapped my hands, a lot!

Soon after, I introduced Bevvy to my beloved Tenerife and we booked into a lovely hotel. We have visited this particular Canary island dozens of times since. Bevvy loves the place and in particular the people she has met over the years in the area known as Costa Adeje. I would love to live there, and so would she, given half a chance

Life was more controlled and manageable by 2010 but there was still my failing health to contend with. In the March of that year I began to see a new GP. I was experiencing breathing problems and coughing fits. The doctor diagnosed me as suffering from acid reflux and had be swallowing gallons of indigestion 'jollop'. This may seem like a minor malady to mention here, but a few months later I was married to Bevvy and our honeymoon in the Maldives Islands was a place where I almost lost my life due to the GP and her misdiagnosis.

I had made money and performed on cruise ships in cabaret in the past but there was no way I wanted to return to cruising. In 2011 a business friend called Jack

Applebaum asked if my employers at *The Stage* would commission an onboard assignment. It was arranged that Bevvy could come along too, and together we joined the gigantic Independence of the Seas cruise ship in the Spanish port of Cadiz. We then had to travel from there back to Southampton and then set off again, where we were scheduled to leave the ship in Lisbon and fly back to the UK.

The Bay of Biscay in the month of February is often referred to as the 'Devil's Dance Floor' and the sea was too rough to put in at Lisbon. We therefore travelled around into the Mediterranean and finally disembarked on the island of Majorca. I really should have warned Bevvy that the sea pass, with which goods and services are paid for whilst passengers are at sea, was connected to my credit card. My lovely wife visited the beauty parlour, where the assistants, working on heavy commission, often ask their customers to try various potions and beauty products. When I received my bill at the end of the cruise, my face must have been a picture.

My dad died at home in his own living room in 2010 and I was away on holiday on Tenerife when he died. An air traffic controllers' strike determined that I was stuck on the island, so I was on the phone a lot to my mother who was urging me to find a way home somehow. My dad had left very exact instructions for his own funeral. Everyone attending was to enjoy a good booze-up and say something nice about him. To my horror I was informed that my sister and her husband, a teetotal chapel-goer, had arranged for tea and a sandwich in the chapel.

When I finally stopped visualising my poor old dad spinning around in his grave, I took control, albeit from a distance on the phone from the Canary Isles. I rang my childhood friend John Hemingway who came to the rescue. The first club that Dad was a member of was in Ryhill. In fact, I discovered later that he had taken a walk around Wakefield and places from his youth just a few days before he died and he had called into this particular club while wandering around on his own one evening.

John rang the club and although they did not open on certain afternoons, they would agree to open to receive mourners at my dad's funeral. Looking back, I now realise I wasted my dad. I could have made much more of his friendship and love while he was alive and when I visited him at the chapel of rest, I took a moment alone with him to thank him for everything. I hope he heard me.

*

39

In 2011 Bevvy and I got married and a great day was had by all. The best man at my first wedding had been a boyhood friend David Pearson. The best man at my second wedding was Tony Wayne.

By then we had someone else very special in our lives. His name was Oscar and he was the most wonderful, loyal and loving Old English sheepdog. some people call them Dulux dogs. Thanks to kind friends, Oscar was able to attend the wedding and Tony Wayne even supplied our beloved boy-hound with a tie.

The show business stagewear tailor Neil Crossland lent us his Bentley as a wedding car and we enjoyed a wedding lunch, followed by an evening party for a larger group of family and friends.

We headed off on honeymoon to the island of Hudhuranfushi, which is one of the hundreds of islands in the Indian Ocean known collectively as the Maldives. No news, no shoes for a fortnight, and one evening Bevvy and I found ourselves sitting next to an English couple. At first the conversation was stilted and awkward. The encounter ended with the distinct impression that the couple Peter and Julie had been sussing us out a little. The result was a friendship which meant such a lot. Julie is Bev's best friend to this day and I became very close with Peter, until his sudden death in 2013. He suffered a heart attack and we visited him when he was on life support at

Scarborough hospital. Sadly, he did not survive. I don't make friendships very easily and Peter's death had a profound emotional effect on me.

Meanwhile back in the Indian Ocean, I was reminded of the year before when I had started seeing a new GP and she began treating me for acid reflux. Despite a history of chest problems, I was never offered a chest X-ray and a spirometry (lung function) test, showed that my breathing was pretty good. Of course, the factor of my being a trained singer and therefore making the most of my respiratory system was never taken into account.

The Maldives are very low-lying islets. Giant bats fly above them and the vegetation, though lush, reminded me of what the end of the world must look like. The place was almost the death of me, as I struggled with breathing difficulties and coughing fits throughout the entire fortnight. One day I visited the doctor's surgery there, a breeze-block structure complete with a tin roof on the beach. The excellent doctor there gave me antibiotics, diagnosing a chest infection, but the night before we were due to leave, we ventured out for dinner from our guest suite on stilts on the sea. I was soon in the company of the doctor again, as I collapsed with what was described as 'cough syncophy'. I had quite literally coughed myself unconscious.

I conned them into letting us fly home early and managed to make my way, slowly through Dubai airport to catch the connecting flight to Manchester. Bevvy immediately took my down to the A&E department at our local hospital, where my chest was X-rayed and a young boy, claiming to be a qualified doctor, informed me there was nothing much wrong with me.

The actor and entertainer Neil Hurst and I had worked together previously in pantomime and shortly after returning from honeymoon, Bevvy and I went along to see Neil playing Wishee Washee in *Aladdin* at the Victoria Theatre in Halifax. I had gone along at the behest of *The Stage* to write a review. Unaware of my illness, Neil was aware that I was in the audience somewhere at this particular performance. He coaxed me up onstage and I stooged for him by being placed in a gunge tank for a sketch involving a Chinese laundry. After the scene, I walked off into the wings and collapsed.

We then headed back to hospital. The A&E consultant was soon by my bedside after another chest X-ray revealed that the previous X-ray had not been viewed properly and that I was in fact suffering pneumonia. I was placed in the high dependency unit at Pinderfields Hospital, where I stayed for ten days and very long nights over Christmas.

On New Year's Eve I was on my way home, but was told that my lung damage was irreparable, as an abscess had formed in my lung due to the delay in an accurate diagnosis and I had no idea if I would ever be able to function again as an entertainer. Bevvy was told during Christmas Eve that things may not end well and she was well aware that widowhood was a distinct possibility.

Bevvy nursed me at home and my agent Gordon Kellett rang every day to see how I was doing. I started work again way too soon in the February of 2012, in a two-act cabaret show at Harehills club in Leeds, along with the singer and dancer Melissa Radway. In short, I was rubbish and the next day I was back in hospital, having suffered a relapse.

We had asked friends at our wedding that, if they wanted to buy us presents, they should instead give us Thomas Cook travel vouchers, as we intended to travel to the tiny West Africa nation of the Gambia for a holiday early in 2012. We booked the Gambia trip just before left on honeymoon for the Maldives. When I was deemed unfit to travel due to becoming ill on honeymoon, the travel agency Thomas Cook, or more specifically their insurance people, refused to give us a refund, alleging we had not been accurate on our insurance coverage. I hope I don't upset too many people when I say that in 2019 when Thomas Cook collapsed, I raised a glass to celebrate the demise of this miserable, money-grubbing band of crooks.

We started work again at Thornwick Bay for another season in March 2012, but I wasn't really up for the job. Over a period of time I began to regain at least some of my strength. A short break on the island of Lanzarote recharged my batteries more than a little.

In the summer of 2012, whilst not at the seaside, we began to socialise with a couple who lived in a neighbouring village, who also owned a couple of caravans at Thornwick Bay. Chris and Sarah Powell were their names.

The friendship revealed to me yet again that it is hard to see into someone's mind. Chris Powell was caught on camera by the internet vigilante group Predator Exposure, when he was filmed in the belief that he was meeting a young boy for sex in Leeds. A lot of evidence was discovered in his car boot and he was convicted as a paedophile and sent to prison in 2015. Powell it later emerged was certainly no friend of mine and for those who believe in karma, his unveiling as a pervert caused a few people to contact me and express their feelings.

A meeting with GPs and the health authority in May 2012 allowed me to vent my spleen a little regarding their failure to spot an illness which could easily have killed me the previous Christmas. Their incompetence also conspired to spoil my wedding day and honeymoon.

I started a court case against the doctors concerned and the hospital, which I lost. Enjoying success in negligence claims against the medical professional is rare. In my experience, our medical friends cover for each other, and justice for those damaged by their incompetence is hard to come by. I did find the whole experience of fronting them out quite cathartic and it was good to know I had managed to find my way under their skin of at least one duplicitous GP who stormed petulantly out of the meeting when I deliberately touched a raw conversational nerve.

*

Although the Thomas Cook people had effectively stolen our honeymoon present of holiday vouchers, we did eventually travel to the Gambia.

This tiny West African nation surrounds the River Gambia, which it takes its name from. I loved the country. It is raw but relaxed and the locals are definitely friendly. At that time a military junta, which has since been deposed, was run by a character called President Jammeh.

The hotel was beautiful and Bevvy and I were accompanied by our new friends Julie and Peter who we had met on honeymoon in the Maldives. Aside from a close encounter for Bevvy with a crocodile while travelling around in a private nature reserve, a great time was had by all.

The friendship which Bevvy and I forged with Peter proved to me irrefutably that there were friends out there who I could trust and we all became very close. They say that travel broadens the mind and I'm so lucky to be able to travel and see the world with my wife and best friend Bevvy.

*

Many show business types state their belief that, after many years in the business, nothing surprises them anymore. Just as I had thought I had reached that point in my life, business enemies of mine, some masquerading as friends, proved to me over a period of just over two years, exactly how much I managed to get just about everything wrong. Perhaps I took my eye off the ball. The fact is that, aside from a few gigs and other bits and pieces, the bulk of my earnings were from the holiday centre business and *The Stage* newspaper. 2013 had been a year of transition. After the tragically premature death of my best ally Ian Sandy, I was asked by the holiday centre to set up my own entertainment consultancy business to look after all things entertainment related at their largest site, Thornwick Bay and Sea Farm holiday centre. From cabarets, bands, entertainment staff, technical assistance, safeguarding and all manner of other responsibilities, I had it covered, or so I thought.

The directors of the company who owned this vast site at that time consisted of two elderly brothers, John and Oxley Waud, and a husband and wife team, Steve and Helen Gibbon. The Waud brothers ran a variety of businesses in the area and were both carpenters by trade. They had the reputation of being very careful and frugal with their money. It is my belief that the Wauds knew the cost of everything and the value of nothing.

There was a mess to clean up in 2013, as the previous year Ian Sandy had engaged a young boy as a member of the entertainment team who was the son of a close friend of Ian's. The lad had left school early and illegally and to my horror I had discovered that he was only just 15 years of age when he had started work the previous summer at the holiday centre. By the following season, by which time I was in charge, the lad was at least legal, but a modicum of popularity had gone to his head and his behaviour had become a huge problem. The rest of the staff were a good bunch of kids, but they clearly missed Ian, as indeed I did myself.

The directors then engaged a new guy, who was the licensee, looking after the venues and bars and at first there was no problem. The new man was a one-man caricature of the worst publicans you could ever meet and he was mad about Elvis Presley. His power-trip behaviour was extraordinary, which resulted in a mass demonstration in the main office one day by the previously happy campers, as over a hundred people stormed in all demanding that this egomaniac should be removed. Despite the clear damage this nutcase was doing, Gibbon asked me what he should do about it. I replied that he must get rid of him as soon as possible, at one stage jokingly suggesting that hiring a hit-man would be able to provide a possible solution. The idiot was ruining everything we had taken years to build up. Gibbon decided to shoot the messenger and the die was cast. My days were numbered.

As well as holding the entertainment contract, I was

still working as an adult room compere. I was tipped off that a former Thornwick Bay entertainment manager had rented a house nearby and had stated his intent to step into my shoes. I was further informed confidentially that a married couple who ran an entertainment agency had attended secret meetings with Gibbon. Suddenly the job had gone from creating a fun atmosphere at a holiday centre to constant tension and pointless intrigue in a place where a number of people had been set against each other. At the end of 2013 season I could and should have walked away. The job was a season-to-season contract and, given the benefit of hindsight, that was the time to go. I made the mistake of staying and fighting it out.

I spent the winter of 2013 and '14 doing the rounds of the clubs as usual, but a meeting in London at the end of January 2014 flagged up the potential for even more business problems in my life.

For the first and as yet only time in my life I was introduced to a man called Hugh Comerford. This was at a show business party in London, which was organised by *The Stage*. Hugh is the brother of Catherine Comerford who had hired me originally at the newspaper. At that juncture Hugh had just been placed in situ as the new managing director. When he was introduced to me, the only impression I gleaned from our brief encounter was of someone whose body language and general demeanour suggested that he did not want to spend any more time with me then he really had to. Comerford seemed rude and abrasive and I perceived that his vision for *The Stage* was of an exclusively London Theatreland publication. He seemed dismissive of every other area of show business.

Later at the same function, my views were reinforced when I chatted with that wonderful actor Timothy West, who decided to let me in on his belief that *The Stage* had lately improved immeasurably. He opined that "not so long ago *The Stage* had turned into a newspaper for variety turns and these days the newspaper is now aimed at actors and theatre people again." Mr West then glanced casually at the badge on my lapel. Everyone was given a badge as part of the reception process. On my lapel the badge read 'MARK RITCHIE – Regional Representative – *The Stage* newspaper'. Timothy then enquired exactly what my role at *The Stage* entailed. I replied; "I write about variety turns."

There were still pleasant and unexpected distractions in my business life. I was invited to a function in London and I found myself in the company of Hollywood A-lister Al Pacino. At the time I had just received a number of injections into my right elbow and Mr Pacino for some reason made a beeline for me and shook my hand rather vigorously. Perhaps he had confused me for someone else? My new friend seemed to notice as I winced visibly during the handshake and a banal conversation followed regarding the merits of a firm handshake. I seldom find myself starstruck but I remember thinking that, if I had known I was going to meet the great Al Pacino I would have thought of something more interesting to say.

After feeling relaxed and rested due to a few weeks away on Tenerife, I was back at Thornwick Bay in the

March of 2014. Meetings with Mr Gibbon were becoming ever more frequent and acrimonious and my all too apparent stress levels were bringing on Bevvy's lachrymose side.

I didn't know it when I walked onstage, but on June 7th 2014 I performed my final show at Thornwick Bay holiday centre. Driving back to Wakefield after my Saturday night show, I presented myself at the local A&E department suffering from chest pains. I had been feeling these types of pain for a while but had said nothing. After a short overnight stay, I was sent home with some medication, with further investigations pending. I had been diagnosed as suffering from angina.

The following day Gibbon rang my home and Bevvy put him on the phone to me. His opening gambit was to ask how I was, as apparently several people at the holiday centre had told him I looked ill. I replied truthfully that I had become ill while at Thornwick but I would soldier on. Gibbon then dropped the bombshell: "I want you out and I want a new cabaret compere now!" He added vehemently and belligerently that he was the client and he was in charge. His next line was when he actually named who he wanted my successor in the job to be. His choice was a singer who was also an entertainment agent, in partnership (or perhaps more accurately in cahoots) with her fellow agent and husband. I put two and two together and heard the penny drop.

The conspiracy was finally revealed and a few days later, on a red-hot day, Bevvy and I, as ever in times of trouble accompanied by Tony Wayne, headed for the site to pick up our belongings and clean out our guest caravan.

Demonstrations organised by holiday caravan owners and a campaign to have me reinstated began immediately. The new compere and her slippery husband moved straight in, before the husband himself was banned from the site for falling out with guests. People posted stuff on social media revealing that the adult venue, which I had worked so hard to build up was often almost deserted and Gibbon's hairbrained scheme was complete. Until the end of the 2014 season I still had a legal contract as entertainment consultant for the site, but I was not allowed to enter the place, even if I wanted to.

About a month or so later, Gibbon rang me unexpectantly. He was laughing down the phone, announcing: that "Elvis has left the building!" The guy behind the bar who had created all the chaos had finally done the right thing and legged it, resigning from the latest in a long line of jobs he didn't seem to be very good at. A holiday centre venue needs a licensee but the guy behind this particular bar was labelled 'Complex Manager', which seemed to give him the belief he had power over everything in sight. I was quite pleased to hear this not entirely unexpected news, but frankly I could not give a toss!

Towards the end of the summer, I happened to be enjoying a few days away in Scarborough with Bevvy. I had heard that this Elvis-loving barman had been put in charge of a pub in the resort. When I walked into the pub, his face was a picture. Watching him carefully, I could see the cogs were whizzing around in his head as he busied himself behind the bar. I'm sure I was the last person he was expecting to see. My motive for the surprise visit was that I had heard he fancied himself as some sort of amateur gangster. I was unimpressed by this man and his boastfulness.

I visited Thornwick Bay holiday centre just one more time, in order to visit the staff. Gibbon tried to string me along, hinting that he may award me the contract for the following season. If he had, I would have taken great delight in telling him where to shove it. The people who took over the contract went to a great deal of trouble in their contribution to my ousting. In the end they gained very little as the holiday centre giant Haven Holidays acquired the site for a reported £29 million at the end of the following season. Those who took such trouble and displayed such an astonishing level of spite and duplicity to remove me, were soon themselves out on their ears.

The day after I received Gibbon's shock phone call informing me that I was heading for the exit door at Thornwick, I had also received a letter from Hugh Comerford. His letter informed me that my services as regional representative at *The Stage* were no longer required. He informed me that if I wanted to pitch content for the newspaper I should contact the editor Alistair Smith. This would have been difficult as for many months before this point, Smith did not reply to my e mails or return my phone calls. In an epic e-mailed reply to Comerford, I pointed out a few home truths, but it was all quite pointless as the die was cast.

Looking back on my time travelling around all over the UK for *The Stage*, I feel nothing but pride. The timing of me receiving my marching orders less than 36 hours after the same fate befell me at the holiday centre seemed shabby and disrespectful.

When I started to regain my strength, I was pleased when I picked up a few cabaret gigs but then a double-whammy financial body blow proved impossible to overcome.

*

—42—

I am told that, when forged later in life, relationships can fall apart easily if the pressure becomes intolerable. In 2015 Bevvy and I had a spell apart. In fact, I instigated the split myself and a couple of friends helped me move Bevvy's belongings out of the house. We were apart for a very short time. We just belong together. Unfortunately, when we make others privy to inside personal and knowledge whilst believing they are trustworthy, mistakes are made and things can become messy. I'm afraid it was me yet again who was guilty of not spotting what was as plain as a pike-staff. Even people we think we know can misplace their moral compass when they discover their loyalties clashing with other interests. Despite hassles on social media and other distractions, Bevvy and I are now stronger as a couple then ever before and we weathered the storms. Thank heavens.

In the spring of 2016, yet another GP managed to get me seen and assessed at Fieldhead hospital in Wakefield. This is a psychiatric establishment with facilities for in-patients, out-patients and a secure unit. My mental health seemed to consist of good days, bad days and even worse days. My lack of control was all too obvious at times when it came to my emotions. I walked away from a number of conflict situations as I was quite literally not responsible for my actions.

There is such a stigma attached to mental health

problems, particularly where I come from, and I found the drive into the car park at Fieldhead quite daunting. In fact I was terrified. Fieldhead is a pretty new facility but the former Stanley Royd hospital stood just down the road from Fieldhead and was the original psychiatric hospital in Wakefield, called the West Riding Pauper Lunatic Asylum. The roadside area, close to where the hospital once stood was referred to then and still to this day as 'Asylum Corner'.

The crushing sense of failure at actually being referred to this place for treatment produced one of the hardest days of my life. I found a space in the already busy carpark and, following the instructions I had been given on foot, I almost turned tail and headed home, as I was convinced that the moment I walked through the door I would be placed in a straitjacket and led straight to the nearest padded cell.

I walked around the corner into the main entrance. Looking across to my right, I saw the secure psychiatric unit with its fences and alarms, designed to keep some patients in and unwanted visitors out. I pressed on and, with leaden feet, I finally pushed myself through the front door. A receptionist pointed me in the right direction and I headed up what looked like a normal hospital corridor. I was surprised to see signs pointing the way to a museum, which contains ghoulish artefacts from the past when mental illness was treated very differently. A buzzer system let me into the adult psychological care unit, and another receptionist showed me into a waiting room. Eventually my therapist, a doctor of psychiatry, came in and beckoned me down another corridor into her consultation room, which resembled more of an office set-up then a hospital. That day I began my journey to self-discovery and eventually I started undergoing a therapy which was facilitated by rapid eye movement and is a form of hypnosis.

Leaving at the end of my first one-hour appointment, I felt like a huge weight had been lifted from me – and this was the first of many such sessions. There is no magic wand that could be waved. This is a process. No psychobabble. No bullshit. Undergoing this treatment requires several prerequisites: courage, an open-mind, total honesty and a recognition that change is necessary.

I returned home that day and told Bevvy that it was official and I was definitely barmy. Bevvy announced that she had known it all along and we laughed and hugged.

I couldn't cope with too much navel-gazing and I got stuck into some hobbies that previously I did not have the time to become too engrossed in.

Tracing my family tree was something I found truly fascinating. I discovered that my paternal ancestors were no strangers to money troubles themselves. The family fortunes had clearly dipped through many generations, from the lofty status of 17th century gentleman land owners, to early 20th century coalminers. There were aliases and moonlight flits as 18th and 19th century family members living in the horse-racing mecca of Newmarket, saw fluctuating fortunes, with census records suggesting a many and varied range of occupations. It seems my ancestors must have been backing all the wrong horses.

My most exciting discovery in genealogy was when my research revealed that I am a direct descendent of the Jacobean playwright John Webster. Young John was a child actor in Philip Henslowe's London company and he was portrayed in the imagination of a rather more modern playwright, Tom Stoppard, in the John Madden film *Shakespeare in Love.*

Virtually off my life I have been fascinated by the Whitechapel murders of 1888. The press dubbed the serial killer Jack the Ripper and the murderer was never identified. Until now.

During some of my 'down time', I decided to get stuck into the research and was pointed in a certain direction simply by an accident peek I took online at some old parish records for Mile End, Stepney, Spitalfields and Whitechapel, all in East London.

It is my intention to publish my research in a future book. I believe that I now hold documentary evidence that the murderer was a Whitechapel workhouse mortuary attendant called Robert Mann. I also uncovered evidence that a mysterious character called Francis Tumblety provided a motive for what I now know to be a total of eight murders and three further attacks on women in the Whitechapel and Spitalfields area between 1888 and 1892.

I have also established that a man who I referred to earlier, as being interred in a cemetery in Brisbane,

Australia, was very much involved in five or possibly six of these attacks, all of which resulted in the deaths of women living in the east end of London. His name was Walter Porriott.

The simple fact is that I believe I have solved the mystery of Jack the Ripper by pressing the wrong button on a computer keyboard, which revealed records providing so many answers.

*

—43—

Time for me to launch a brand-new national light entertainment niche publication, marketed in a brand-new way. The idea was to charge a modest annual subscription, but to deliver much more than a monthly magazine. Five years on *UK Cabaret* now has a small but dedicated subscriber list who all receive business support, a jobs section and plenty of opportunities to appear in editorial/advertorial content.

Although some people, for reasons best known to themselves, still do not support *UK Cabaret*, I would say that the classy, glossy, well-designed monthly magazine, which we deliver many hundreds of copies of every month, is not to be sniffed at nowadays.

In 21st century niche publishing, there is a balancing act between the printed word and an online presence. Our web guru Martin Brown, who was been with me since the very beginning, tells me the numbers of unique visitors who look at our website once a week or more are staggering. Adam Press, who is our designer, really is quite a talent and what he produces is both classy and clever.

The big picture in terms of launching our brand spanking new publication in 2016 is that I was back in my playpen. I love show business. I love to see talented people displaying their talents. I love the scene. I love the involvement.

The monthly print and distribution bill for *UK Cabaret* is bloodcurdlingly high and paying for reviewers and contributors really is a stretch some months, but I make the decisions and more than anything, I love to be in control of my own destiny.

*

44

Some people I have known for years have been more important in my life during recent times. Barrie and Vicci Lucas are a husband and wife agency team who run their company from offices in Blackpool. Barrie is notorious for being close with his money and business savvy, favouring representing performers who are smart, slick and often performing soul and Motown music.

He saw an opening to present national showcase events. *The Stage* had misguidedly stopped running Showcall Showcase and Barrie seems able to attract all the major cabaret bookers and agents to his events. This means that the acts and bands, who pay to showcase themselves, can be seen and possibly booked by a huge and varied list of attendees, from the cruise ship, club, events and holiday centre markets. The way they operate is simple. Vicci provides the brains and the glamour, Barrie sells and has more front than the town of Blackpool where he lives. Their company Showcase Productions is big business and I am delighted to be involved with them. There are two other such national events, one staged by a company in Southend-on-Sea. The organisers are vigorous and clever and I enjoy attending their annual showcase.

When I was axed at *The Stage*, the Facebook keyboard warriors went into overdrive. Some were venting their spleen by stating publicly how pleased they all were that

I had received the bullet. I don't think any of them envisaged me bouncing back yet again when I launched *UK Cabaret* magazine. There were one or two red faces when certain people saw me doing the rounds up and down the country trying to provide a voice and a platform of publicity for light entertainment in our country. I just got on with the project instead of indulging myself in what would have been a well justified spot of gloating. Most of those doing their little trolling thing on Facebook had become involved in another showcase event called Keeping it Live. This event passes me pretty much unnoticed as, for reasons best known to the organisers, they actually shun publicity. As none of this small band of showbusiness renegades support or subscribe to *UK Cabaret*, I regard our absence from their event with some relief. They don't invite us, we don't wish to attend. They don't support us, we don't support them. That's just how it is. By not attending we save money on paying for reviewers and magazine space, which can't be bad. Apparently, we are not wanted by the people at Keeping it Live, and that is fine with me.

We took Oscar for his last holiday in Whitby in 2018 and by then our boy hound seemed to be slowing down quite a bit, as he trotted with us on the beach, on our favourite route from Whitby west cliff and the coastal village of Sandsend. I think there is probably no more loyal and trusting friend than a good dog.

He kept going for another ten months, but our vet told us he had a form of leukaemia and he was feeling fairly grotty for most of the time. Eventually the spark went out of his eye and one morning, I took him for a final stroll on Heath Common, close to where we live. He indicated that he wanted to go back to the car and Bevvy and I took him to the vet and soon later he was gone. I kissed his head and he went off for his final sleep.

Oscar was an integral part of my mental illness therapy. He was a huge light in my life when things could not have been much worse. I have tears in my eyes as I write this. He was my big boy. My beautiful boy, my fine splendid boy and I truly loved him. Once at home I sobbed uncontrollably at the sheer sense of loss. That night I dreamed that he visited me in my sleep. For a short while I could smell his warm breath and feel his big heart beating.

Trying to be funny at such times is challenge. I was booked for an afternoon gig at a club quite close to where I live. I thought the job would come as a distraction to the sense of desolation I felt after losing Oscar. I arrived at what was a show provided by a club committee to their members, just after their annual general meeting. I noted it was a family audience and material was no problem.

What was a problem was that one of the club officials had brought a bunch of toddlers and had sat right at the front of the stage. I began trying to perform stand-up comedy, while the kids were running around the stage area, trying the climb on to the stage and generally whooping and hollering on the dance floor right in front of me. Most parents would have the manners and the common sense to keep the kids close by. After all is said and done, we are entertainers and not babysitters.

At first, I didn't react, but eventually any performer reaches the point when this real mood-killer is (a) distracting the audience who want to hear the show, and (b) we look at the parents necking food and guzzling drinks while their little monsters run riot and eventually we think, stuff this! I started with a few innocuous comments aimed at the parents but they clearly weren't listening. Then I threw in a verbal volley of sarcasm as I told the parents directly from the stage: "It's okay folks, don't worry about your kids knackering my show up. You just sit there getting pissed and I'll amuse the little darlings for you!" The whole group promptly got up and left. Some people from the audience told me after the show that I had done the right thing, but the agent who supplies their acts was told by the club's representatives not to send me to the club again. To be honest, I was delighted.

By 2017 *UK Cabaret* was covering large-scale events, with everything from the Royal Variety performance to the National Tribute Music Awards being featured. The appeal of what is offered to readers consists of reviews, features and advertising. *UK Cabaret* is a work in progress.

I had visited the Edinburgh Festival Fringe when at *The Stage* years before. Many of the reviewers back then were people I had frankly never even heard of, so I have no idea if they engage anyone with the credentials required to view, appraise or critique stand-up comedy. After obtaining the obligatory press accreditation, I took Bevvy for her first visit to the fringe in 2017. The Edinburgh festival is massive and I love the atmosphere generated at the fringe. Walking the streets gives access to the Free Fringe, where I have experienced shows which entertain, bamboozle, bewilder or just drift past me.

It wasn't Bevvy's scene, even though I have seen some amazing comedy talent from Larry Dean to Eddie Izzard and from Katherine Ryan to Camilla Cleese (daughter of John Cleese). At the 2018 and 2019 fringes, I went up on my own and met all kinds of people, but it's not the same without my best friend at my side. Curiously, Bevvy's interest in the great city of Edinburgh is centred around the existence of Greyfriars Bobby and the fact that the zoo houses giant pandas. Both of these attractions don't really provide much interest for *UK Cabaret* readers.

Returning to my own stage act, I decided in 2017 to come up with something a bit different. After coming up with new material, I put a showreel on my website and changed my billing to 'Mark Ritchie – A Fat Old Comic Who Sings a Bit'. The description came from a Facebook keyboard warrior who was having a bit of a go at me after reading a review he didn't like. Although meant as an insult, I love the description, so I kept it. Perfect!

In late 2016 my mum suffered a stroke. The biggest effect was on her memory, which until her death in 2019 she tried hard to cover up. The only reason I am still here now is that when I was at my lowest ebb in 2015, Mum bailed me out financially and for that I am always grateful. Mum met my dad at the Unity Hall in Wakefield at a dance in 1950. They were inseparable and, despite my sister selling my mum a house right next door to where she lived, Mum was lonely, bored, forgetful and drank far too much alcohol My sister's second husband is a widower who lived in the house next door. When Dad died in 2010 Mum was persuaded to buy my sister's house, which was a decision I know Mum later regretted bitterly.

On the Clubland front, I was presented with a life achievement award in November 2017. While it was nice to receive the award, I'm pretty sure I know that my friend, the great club man Brian Cunningham was very much behind the decision to recognise me in this fashion.

In November of 2017 I was invited to a swanky affair in London's Park Lane, at the Grosvenor House Hotel. The Grand Order of Water Rats is a very old and eminent show business organisation. Their London headquarters in Grays Inn Road houses a show business museum, which is paradise to an anorak like me. The group raises pots of money for charity and their female counterparts are the Lady Ratlings. They are just as prolific in their fundraising activities as the men. If you reverse the letters of RATS, you can find the explanation as to the name adopted in the Victorian music hall era by this amazing organisation.

The King Rat is a title awarded to outstanding members of the fraternity every year. King Rat 2017 was that fine comedian Ian Richards and on the night Bevvy and I were honoured to be his guests. We were seated next to members of Ian's lovely family and close to Queen legend Brian May and his wife the actress Anita Dobson. Also close by was comedian Jimmy Tarbuck and the wonderfully warm and witty Nicholas Parsons, who became King Rat himself just before his own death early in 2020. We were indeed in fine company and we have been invited every year since by the Water Rats administrator Anthony Bohan and the Scribe Rat Mike Martin who, amidst a multitude of other show business roles he performs, now works with us at *UK Cabaret* as a show reviewer. The longest Water Rats ball we attended was when TV presenter Eamonn Holmes was being presented with an award. Eamonn droned on for almost an hour to a late-night audience who demonstrated their sheer delight when he finally sat down and legged it.

*

45

One of the few advantages of travelling all over the country as an entertainer or entertainment writer is the sightseeing opportunities provided. My interests are many, with the First World War being a particular focus over the years, due mainly to both my grandfathers' involvement. One fought in the trenches at Ypres, while the other sailed across the Irish Sea in 1916, during the time of the Irish Easter Rising.

In times of my life when the stress has been blanket-bombing my head, I go and hide in a book or a film. Reading poetry is a great comfort. John Betjeman is my favourite. I have a huge library, but I don't read much fiction. Biography and history are my favourites.

A long time ago I read about a man called Percy Toplis, who was a member of the Royal Army Medical Corps during the Great War. Toplis was quite a slippery customer and he was once sought by the Secret Service as he became Britain's most wanted man at the end of the War in 1918.

I knew that Toplis was brought up by his aunt and uncle in the pit village of Blackwell in north Nottinghamshire. Like many Victorian pit villages, there was original housing from when the places were first settled and rows of terraced housing were sometimes added later for the miners and their families, once the pits were sunk. On my way to a show one summer's evening, I drove into what remains of Blackwell, stumbling on the tiny place, quite by accident. A few enquiries revealed the location of the old pit housing. It is now flattened and the land seems to be occupied mainly by allotments. The location of the old pit, where Toplis went down as an apprentice blacksmith in 1910, is well marked and there is a methane drainage facility, as the gas in some cases still seeps to the surface from old mine workings.

The Monocled Mutineer was a soubriquet identifying Toplis and his supposed part in the so-called Etaples Mutiny by British soldiers in France in 1917. Some of the evidence against him is questionable to say the least, but he was certainly someone who grew up in surroundings that he didn't feel part of and I empathised with that.

Toplis was eventually shot dead while in the run in an area close to the Scottish border. His death was bizarre. His short life was that a conman and loveable rogue. The writer Alan Bleasdale adapted the story for television from a book by John Fairley and William Allison, and Paul McGann played the part of Toplis.

The four-part adaption was first shown in 1986 and, after a huge furore, created mainly by Tory grandees, the series has never been repeated. Almost 35 years after *The Monocled Mutineer* was made and over a hundred years after the Great War ended, it seems there are still people around who wish to rewrite history.

As I left Blackwell that evening, my thoughts were of the con-man who was so revered by his comrades in the trenches because he managed to inject some fun and laughter making the whole experience a little less traumatic. The ghost of Percy Toplis is said to haunt the Blackwell Hotel pub. Perhaps villages like Blackwell remain full of the ghosts from all our pasts.

*

46

In the eyes of some people, I don't even fit into show business and never have. There are some who see me a certain way and can't see beyond their perception of me as a person. This factor is often reflected in my stage work and can be bad for business if certain people choose not to hire me or engage with me just because they don't like the part of myself I choose to reveal.

The actors and entertainer's union Equity hold a variety show for charity every year in Leeds and their leading light is lovely lady called Valerie Mann. Valerie is a children's entertainer who goes by the name of Mrs Tipsy. She is also an Equity official. In 2017 Valerie asked me to take part in the show staged at a nice club in Leeds and I was happy to accept. On the night, the other acts included the Grumbleweeds, a very popular lady in Clubland circles by the name of Little Sam Lyons, and my friend Tony Wayne. I thought my own spot went reasonably well and from the stage I informed the crowd that I had not been on the stage at that particular club since 1991, when the previous man in charge, a lovely bloke called Paul Ford, had booked me in a show which marked his own retirement.

I remember being nervous that night back in 1991, as everyone who was anyone in Clubland was seated out front in the packed room. One of my own comedy heroes Peter Wallis was out there that night. Known as

'Machine-Gun Wallis' due to the sheer speed of his stand-up comedy delivery, Peter was often seen as an actor on telly, popping up frequently as a customer in Ronnie Barker's corner shop sit-com *Open All Hours*.

These days I am not welcome for some reason at this particular club. I am excluded from the normal scheduled concert nights, which are booked by the people in charge there. There is no point in sweating over the small stuff. That's life. My life.

When we try and make a living in the insular world of Northern Clubland we will always find managers, agents and club officials who eagerly book us and those who do not. There are only ever three reasons why some entertainers don't find regular work:

1. Your act is simply not good enough
2. You cause problems in terms of temperament or general behaviour whilst out working.
Or 3. You don't pay your commission to the agents.

The only caveat outside of the three reasons above is when the artiste has sufficient profile to make his/her name noteworthy somehow in a negative way. This is most usually when a potential booker just does not personally like a particular entertainer.

Venue-goers have no idea of the politics involved with in the booking of live entertainment and perhaps this is a good thing. Entertainment agents control large swathes of what remains of the club scene. Control of what goes on holiday park stages is normally a stitch-up, involving people who used to work in some capacity on the parks and it is all a bit of an old-pals act. There is nepotism in many areas of business but the sheer scale of show business insider dealing is most evident when the business coalesces for meetings and get-togethers most commonly held at trade showcase events, which of course the public are not invited into.

There are a number of people whose names I could reel off instantly who have been around the business a long time but have never hit the big time. There are others whose rise is meteoric and, in my view, in many cases thoroughly undeserved.

I have been around all areas of show business for most of my life, but I can say with great honesty that I still have very little idea on the subject of how and why the business works in the way it does. Perhaps that's what makes it so fascinating.

*

47

In June 2018, on Father's Day, I ended up very nearly making a fool of myself whilst performing a routine show at the Clarence club in York. My memories were making me emotional, just seconds before I was due to walk onstage.

This social club at the Clarence is said to be haunted, with many visiting entertainers claiming to have seen apparitions in the dressing room. The stage is an old-fashioned winged affair, with a few steps at the back, stage left, where entertainers have to duck their heads to avoid the low doorway.

As it was Father's Day, I remember finding myself deep in thought while recalling vividly a previous visit to the same club in in 1995, I had dropped my son off for a hospital visit, as his ears needed to be fitted with grommets. His mum stayed with him in hospital and with an absence of babysitters around, I took my daughter to work. Kids weren't allowed in the club, so I made a comfortable and safe nest for my daughter in the dressing room where a kind club official supplied her with pop and crisps etcetera.

If you are telling gags on a stage and people laugh in the wrong places, it normally means either your flies are undone – or something is happening on the stage behind you. I looked around quickly, only to find my eight-year-old daughter sitting on the steps at the back of the stage in full view of one side of the audience. My daughter was a real daddy's girl back then.

As we get older, those of us lucky enough to still have our parents around have to realise eventually that we must be ready to deal with their inevitable loss. Bevvy's dad was Gerald Wood, a retired engineer and keen crown green bowler. Gerald died in late 2017 and immediately money began to appear from everywhere. He had accounts no one was even aware of. There were trust funds, shares galore, and large amounts of high denomination bank notes were eventually discovered all over the house. Gerald always pleaded poverty and used to live frugally and thriftily. In any event, a full-scale search through everything from the linings of his clothes to the turn-ups in his trousers, produced many thousands of pounds.

Sad news comes and goes. The memories linger and the grandchildren come along. They create new memories and the circle of life keeps turning.

By 2018, I had submitted a weekly column for the local papers every single week for 33 years. I just gave up one day and my column was never replaced. Even after a third of a century, I didn't expect a marching band or a golden handshake. In the event I received absolutely nothing. Nada. Zilch. Not even a thank-you letter. The company I had signed on for all those years ago no longer existed and had been acquired a decade before by the sprawling conglomerate that is Johnson Publishing. The bean-counters had taken over. The local newspapers had lost their soul, their aim and much of their readership.

There were reports last year of the difficulties this company was in and I wasn't surprised in the very least.

Making money performing in the clubs was becoming increasingly tough. Political correctness was creeping in, even with many of the older club members. We live in a world now where everyone seems to feel a sense of entitlement when it comes to becoming offended. I'm now convinced that some people come out in order to moan about something or other and claiming to be offended by a joke is the new antidote to laughter and fun.

My least favourite clubs include Kirkheaton Conservative club in Huddersfield, Keighley Liberal club and Albion Street club in Castleford. There are however lots of other venues where a miserable minority spoil the atmosphere for the majority with their apparent willingness to become offended at just about anything and everything.

Maltby Catholic club near Rotherham is a lovely venue, but a booking for a special club members' night late in 2018 presented me with quite a challenge. I was booked alongside singer and comedian Johnnie Martell, who opened the show. The guest of honour was the local Catholic priest who, at that time, had only just taken over his new Yorkshire patch after arriving from his native Zimbabwe. This chap came along and gave Martell and I a bit of a pep talk before the show.

Apparently, the same function the year before was the priest's first visit to the club. Whoever was onstage that night clearly located a nerve quite some distance away from the funny bone of the good Father. His response was to give the entertainer a jolly good talking to after the show. Martell, normally quite a cheeky chappie, stuck to singing and I went out and performed what I call my 'posh cruise-ship spot', which contains not a single swearing utterance and material of the clean and clever variety. The priest did not complain and I made the assumption all was well. I swept up the comedy eggshells I had been walking on straight after the show.

Our lovely friend Julie and my Bevvy have been very close for some years now, but three years after the death of Julie's original partner Peter, Julie found love again with her present partner. Tony is an ex-serviceman divorcee who clearly loves Julie dearly. When together we are indeed a happy foursome.

In 2018 my son Steven married his Amy. They are as thick as thieves and obviously devoted to each other. The wedding day itself was wonderful. On the big day, Bevvy and I went along to the registry office and we took my mum, who by then wasn't too sure what was going on due to her dementia which was triggered by the stroke. I was pleased and proud to be there for my son and at the reception, Bevvy, Mum and I were seated with Amy's parents and grandparents. It was a lovely afternoon. We didn't stay for the evening party, when all Steven and Amy's friends came along. We had Mum to think of. I am immensely proud of my son and the man he has become. I still dream of walking my daughter down the aisle one day. Who knows, perhaps?

*

—48—

When my agent Gordon Kellett died, I knew decisions had to be made, which turned out to be much easier than I imagined. Gordon's daughter Tracey Gunney is cut from the same cloth as her dad and she continues to handle my live performance work diary. I produced a huge variety show in Gordon's honour, which was a massive success.

There are less and less venues that want to book a fat, old comic who sings a bit these days. Cabaret and club work are not plentiful for anyone of course, but some of the agents and club officials seem to labour under the misapprehension that by putting young performers on stages they will attract younger people in through the doors. This is complete cobblers of course, but it means that, unbelievably, for some of the Clubland decision-makers I am simply too old now. As hard as it may be to believe, even in 2020, Tracey still finds a few nice gigs for me.

In late 2019 I was approached to take part in *Britain's Got Talent*. Firstly, a researcher 'facebooked me' out of nowhere and starting blowing smoke up my backside. This person more or less told me I was the next comic genius and she had been watching my showreel on my website. Her boss (some sort of producer) had agreed that I should be invited PDQ to the London Palladium for a live audition in front of the Cowell talent mafia, where I could take off like a comedy rocket.

I was curious so I played along just to find out what lengths these people were willing to go to in putting together what I believe to be the most exploitative and tatty programme on TV. Promises were made, which I cannot outline here as they were made verbally on my mobile phone so I cannot prove what was said. There was no contact for a while, then the whole Palladium thing, which was due to be filmed on my birthday, was suddenly cancelled and I was instructed instead to go to a rehearsal hall somewhere near Nottingham. I declined the invitation. Perhaps the *BGT* people cooled their interest in making me into a comedy superstar when they dug a little and discovered my associations in the press.

In any event I certainly have no desire to be famous. In fact, if the date had been set for me to appear on this apology for television light entertainment, I would have replied that I would rather share a jacuzzi with Susan Boyle while red-hot pokers were being forcibly inserted into my bum. In short, it's not for me. Cowell himself has made his opinions on cruise cabaret artistes abundantly clear and I have seen too many people emerge from the *BGT* experience with their professional reputations damaged, in some cases irreparably.

As I mentioned before, once I had lost all my income from the holiday centre and *The Stage* in 2015 I also seemed to lose what I now laughingly refer to as 'friends'. Aside from a precious few they were all gone, virtually overnight. I was described by one person as "a busted flush", with my best days behind me. According to many naysayers, I was finished and that was that.

I occasionally ponder on the successful emergence of my new magazine and web business. Perhaps so many of these 'friends', who apparently believed a few years ago that I was excluded from their sphere of influence are now feeling pretty silly. In any event. I don't care. They don't matter to me anymore. My entire life revolves around Bevvy, my two Old English sheepdogs Stan and Ollie, my son and grandchildren, my work on *UK Cabaret*, plus of course a few live gigs and my hobbies.

Despite my life being more a narrow and insular affair these days, a few years ago I found myself picking up on an old friendship, which has provided Bevvy and I with a great social outlet. Maggie Mills is a local pub landlady and a dear friend. Bevvy has made many friends amongst the regulars of Maggie's pub in the small town of Normanton, close to the village where we live. My wife is much-liked and loved and I tag along and enjoy the camaraderie. Within an area, which is known for being close-knit, we have been accepted into the fold and that speaks volumes.

I have pulled a few strokes in my time and I have been lucky, so lucky to survive in the shark-infested waters that have provided me with a living for so long. My old friend Howard Burnette once said of me: "If you weren't so honest, you would have made a great con-man. You could find your way out of a room with no doors." In 2018 I found myself in a situation that, try as I might, I could not find my way through the woods, due to some pretty thick and thorny trees.

*

In March 2018 yet another tragedy unfolded, when we took Bevvy's mum on holiday to Tenerife. Bevvy ended up spending eight weeks on the island, hoping for Wendy to recover from a variety of serious illnesses, which all reared up simultaneously and eventually took her life on May 5th.

I travelled back and forth, fitting work commitments in between supporting Bevvy, who was to spend eight weeks on Tenerife. Bevvy's mum Wendy died in Mahon hospital in the south of the island and she was cremated locally soon after. Her ashes are now contained in an urn at our home along with Bevvy's dad's and my beloved Old English sheepdog Oscar.

While in the midst of writing this book, I kept asking Bevvy if a reader may think us jinxed. My wife is usually right about most things and, as she points out, tragedy followed yet more misfortune and bad luck followed misadventure time and time again.

Not long after Wendy's death, there was an incident on the M1, when the fire brigade cut me out of my Mercedes car, after a wheel simply fell off the vehicle whilst driving home from a show. I managed to bring the vehicle to a stop on the hard shoulder somehow and off I went to hospital. Tony Wayne jumped into his car and quickly came out and dealt with the aftermath for me, while I popped off to A&E to be checked over. In the view of a policeman who inspected the wreck, the only possible explanation was that someone had deliberately loosened the wheel nuts and left them just hanging on by a thread. A more paranoid man may consider this as attempted murder. The car I drive today is a very large SUV-type vehicle and the whole unit would have to be removed in order to loosen a wheel. I always check around the car now before every single journey.

Some things cannot be foreseen or prevented and on July 19 2018, I was driving back late at night from a business appointment on the Lincolnshire coast, in the resort of Skegness. At that time, I was driving a Vauxhall car and around midnight I was negotiating the twisting roads, when a set of headlights seemed to fly out of nowhere, over the brow of a hill. As an entertainer, I have been driving home from different shows for years and up to then, I had always managed to dodge the many drunk drivers who cause so much carnage. That night my luck ran out.

A drunk, driving a company van, which he should not even have had access to, smashed into a car in front of me, sending the innocent driver of that vehicle into hospital with life-threatening injuries. With a dense gorse bush hedge effectively fencing me in, there was no way out and I was hit almost head on. I was cut out of the car and the drunk driver, who tried to run from the scene, was arrested shortly after. I went off to hospital with injuries to my legs and hip. Much surgery was required, some of which I am still waiting for. It could have been a lot worse for me. The drunk driver, who it later emerged had considerable previous form in the field of fuckwittery, went to jail and, as I write this tale of woe, my solicitor is still doing her thing and trying to get me compensated.

*

—50—

Early in 2019, my mum was visibly reaching her end. The last time Mum saw me perform was at the Academy Theatre in Barnsley on February 8th that year. She was there in body at least, as by then the real person had already left the building.

On April 14th, Mum died at home. After paying a visit and saying goodbye to the pal of my cradle days, I was straight off to work at a social club in nearby Barnsley. I'm a professional entertainer. It's what I do. Mum's funeral took place and, aside from a handful of real friends – John Hemingway, Roger Auty and Brian Cunningham – no one else came. Tony Wayne could not attend due to illness. There was family present of course, but oddly enough all from my dad's side of the family. I do not know why no one came from my mum's side.

I kept asking myself why I wasn't feeling the type of grief that people told me I was apparently meant to experience. I can't explain. My only feeling was that of being frozen in a bubble of self-preservation. My lack of reaction was my biggest noticeable reaction. My sister and I have always had a volatile relationship. It's hard to say why, but an undignified shouting match with her on the day before Mum died remains my abiding memory of that time.

My mum's ashes were interred along with my dad's at

Ryhill cemetery on June 12th in a plot occupied by my brother who had succumbed to meningitis all those years before.

I was still feeling grief and was missing my dog Oscar more than ever. Dogs are such a comfort. Looking around a certain social networking site which Old English sheepdog lovers engage with, all bitten by the doggie lovebug that breed seems to engender, Bevvy spotted a litter of pups which attracted our interest. On June 4th – by which time I was driving Bevvy's dad's old car – we headed for South Wales and a tiny picturesque village close to the resort town of Porthcawl.

Clevis Hill, with its church, village green, villa-like houses and olde-worlde pubs resembles the type of picture postcard location they chose for films about England in the 30s.

We stayed overnight in a beautiful old house whose owner, a lady called Jane, lets out a few of the bedrooms to the more discerning traveller. Jane is what I call an old money person. What I mean by this expression is that, in my experience, family members from those with historic wealth don't generally put on airs and graces and there is seldom even a hint of snobbishness. Jane's home suggests nothing but impeccable taste and she provides the warmest of warm welcomes.

The following morning, we knocked on the door of a house in nearby Bridgend and immediately fell in love. Mum and dad, namely Darwin and Kiki, had accidently played a bit of jig-a-jig shortly after being introduced and the result was eight adorable puppies. Two of the boy-pups seemed particularly close and we decided to take them, both of them.

We arranged to return to South Wales once the boys were ready to leave their mum, and in the meantime, we headed off with a richly deserved holiday to the Greek island of Thassos. Travelling with us were our friends Julie and Tony, and after everything that had happened, I was desperate for a stress-free break. A frantic phone call from Zoe, the owner of Darwin and Kiki, produced a fair amount of stress for us, whilst on Thassos. One of our pups had apparently swallowed an object and required emergency surgery. Our puppy survived the surgery and all was well.

Bevvy's daughters from her previous marriage have produced some lovely kids themselves. They are not my blood of course but I am the nearest thing to a grandad they have. Bev's daughter Natalie works for the NHS and has done well for herself professionally in the field of physiotherapy. Her oldest child is Shannon and she came along with us to South Wales to pick up the two new loves in our life. We named them Stan and Ollie, mainly due to my love for Laurel and Hardy. We booked into Jane's place to break the journey back and Shannon was soon installed in a luxury suite of her own, which seemed to go down well, as it would with any 14-year-old.

We now have two fully-grown and extremely large and loving dogs sharing our small bungalow in Yorkshire. We are content. Perfect.

*

51

The constant pain of the hip and knee injuries have required the assistance of some pretty heavy-duty pain relief. A business trip to Spain in September of 2019 did not go well. I was still on the NHS waiting list for surgery. Attending a show business trade showcase event in the bustling resort of Benidorm, the pain in my back, hip and knee was off the scale. I knew at that time that I was due to go under the knife for a full knee joint replacement back in the UK the following week.

Lunching with the singer Jennie Castell, who I have become friends with recently, in a seafront restaurant next to the beach, I twisted my knee awkwardly and I felt my hip slip out of place. Knowing Benidorm so well, I did not want to stay in the middle of all the action. Instead I booked into a small hotel right on the beach, in the small, neighbouring coastal town of Cala Finestrat. Returning to my hotel after lunch, I went a bit OTT on the painkillers and fell into a deep dark sleep. I only just woke in time to go off to the showcase.

The following week I rocked up, as arranged, to a hospital where I had attended a pre-operative assessment a few weeks before. Part of the assessment was being forced to admit the triggers for my post-traumatic stress disorder. It became obvious once I went into hospital that the nurse at the assessment hadn't been listening.

Due to my final accident down Nostell colliery all those years before, one of the triggers which produces what I am now told to describe now as 'panic attacks', is the feeling that my legs are trapped. An anaesthetist, armed with high opinion of himself and impaired by a rather unfortunate attitude, revealed suddenly that I would not be receiving a general anaesthetic. Instead I was informed that a spinal block injection would be administered, resulting in me being awake for the entire surgery. The experience would be that of feeling nothing below the waist. I asked: "Have I any choice in this?" Doctor Wonderful replied tartly as he made his exit: "None whatsoever."

A theatre nurse followed this no doubt esteemed member of the medical profession into the room and I decided to make a stand. The doctor soon returned into the room and I gave him some rather complicated advice regarding what he could do with his stethoscope.

Referred back to my GP, I was then told I would be having the surgery three months later at my own local hospital. I was by then prepared and reconciled with the reality of receiving of receiving the spinal epidural form of anaesthesia I had earlier panicked about and rejected. By then I understood the concerns about my respiratory illness.

I waited and waited, only to be informed the week before the due date that a vomiting bug had swept through the hospital, which was all widely reported in the local press. With patients projectile vomiting willy-nilly, all admissions were postponed and even hospital visitors were banned as no doubt a massive mopping-up operation was taking place.

Another three months elapsed and my surgeries, along with those of the rest of the world, were postponed indefinitely. Covid-19 had arrived and the world hit the collective pause button.

*

52

Covid-19 is the new reality and as I write these words, I wonder if things will ever be the same again.

Unable to do much in the way of stage work and with *UK Cabaret* only making a modest profit thus far, I'm not a wealthy man. The publication as a whole makes money, but designers and web experts have to be paid for. Contributors have to be paid for and the monthly print bill and distribution costs are bloodcurdlingly high for someone with very little additional income other than a few pension investments.

My travelling and general stage work have declined for some time now. Aside from the financial hit, the truth is that the setting up of heavy and cumbersome PA systems and the other accoutrements of stage work and carrying it all in and out of clubs where access conditions are poor have become difficult given my health and mobility problems. In any event the work simply isn't out there today.

During January 2020, around my birthday on the 21st, I began to feel ill. I was breathless, aching and generally feeling pretty grim. Given my respiratory history, the occasional chest infection is very much part of my life. The symptoms of this episode however were slightly different and I only worked onstage sporadically. Bevvy was ill too. We now believe we may both have contracted this dreadful virus Covid-19 at that time.

Before the lockdown, funds were very low to start with, but after a larger than usual run of business expenses pertaining to *UK Cabaret* during the lockdown month of March, the cupboard was bare.

Enter the force of nature in human form that is Joanne Speight. Joanne is a social worker for the local authority, but that statement alone is perhaps comparable to describing a beauty queen as 'quite pretty'. Joanne is someone who wants to change the world for the better and for those who are fortunate enough to be her friend, Joanne's friendship and loyalty is total and unconditional. When Bevvy and I were both ill, Joanne did so much, from practical help and advice to just being there, 24/7.

Ignoring the advice of some, throughout the lockdown I have been writing these words. I have tried for the very first time in my life to be completely honest. If my candour seems inappropriate or downright odd to the reader, I'm sorry.

But I don't owe anyone in showbusiness a brass farthing and I never have. All I have is the life I have led.

As I put the finishing touches to the telling of this story, I know I have lived through profound and far-reaching changes to our society. From the old traditional industries to the birth of the internet. From the close-knit communities who worked together and played together to the diminution of brotherhood, sisterhood and neighbourhood.

The world we live in is so, so different to the world I was born into back in 1959. I have never felt comfortable in my own skin, so one day I thought that if I didn't like myself the way I was, I would simply invent someone else. I took the new person on to the stage with me and I estimate that, as a performer, producer or compere, I have been involved in excess of 10,000 performances.

As I write these final paragraphs, I am looking forward to returning to the stage again. I have not ventured on to any sort of stage since March 7, 2020, when I appeared at a club in Retford Nottinghamshire. I have been revising and updating material and trying to remember what I do and in which order.

It is now late August and I am soon finally heading into the hospital. The NHS have hired operating theatre facilities in this area at a private hospital location and I am booked in for a six-night stay for joint replacement surgery due to the damage caused by a certain drunk driver.

It is the morning of August 19th and I am also finally returned to the stage this very evening. This is what I do. Bouncing back has become an impulse. A way of life.

As I pack the car with my stage equipment for the first time in so many months, this is quite an adrenaline rush. I admitted to Bevvy that I was apprehensive in doing a job again that has come so easy for me for so long. Coincidentally I am heading to entertain at a club mentioned earlier in this book, the Clarence club in York. Equipment is unloaded in a back alleyway at the club which is situated very close to the factory business built up by the 19th century Quaker, philanthropist and chocolatier Joseph Rowntree. A small passageway leads towards a few steps which rise to an old-fashioned winged stage. The concert hall is very long indeed and when full it holds around 350 people.

At the appointed time I walk out on stage, after being introduced by the compere. The concert room looks different with a one-way system being indicated to those present by a series of directional stickers on the wooden floor of the auditorium. It is operating with waiter/waitress service only and a log is kept of anyone entering. The room is pretty busy, despite the spaced-out seating arrangement and I'm ready to go.

I feel like it is the first time all over again. I pause just to try and remember who this fellow Mark Ritchie is and what makes him entertaining.

I try not to look under the spotlights at the faces of the audience. I focus on doing my opening song and launching myself properly and effectively into my opening salvo of patter.

Lo and behold I can do it. I remember almost all of it all just the way it was and I am well received by an audience sitting at their individual tables and observing social distancing. It seems many are just glad to be back out at the club at all, resuming club life and their social outlet.

After the gig, I drive into the night, out of the historic city centre of York and out towards the A64 which will provide my route home. Straight away I drop back into my old night-time driving habit of watching for the bobbies and the bad guys. I play the gig back in my head trying to accentuate the positive within the imagined dialogue I hear in my head.

After my previous close encounter with the drunk driver I still feel an acute sense of anxiety at night driving, but using money left by Bevvy's mum in her will, I am now driving the large and powerful SUV-type car that Bevvy bought me with cash last Christmas Eve. The car is an automatic, so no pain in my left knee as there is no clutch to operate.

Despite the new reality of Covid-19, I am doing something which has always come reasonably easy to me. I am entertaining live faces. I am someone else for a while. This is the life I have led and like any dinosaur, I will stick around until I have outlived my usefulness.

I have a handful of true friends in the world which is more than some people can say. I reflect on this as I consider the conclusions I have drawn from writing this book. I have tried to make some sense of the often chaotic life I have led, but can find very little by way of rhyme or reason to it all. I hope I have done more good than harm to the nice people, and I hope someday to be able to comprehend why I have apparently made so many enemies. After all, I think I may just have come off worst in the game of life, being so often in the right place but at the wrong time.

All I have is the life I have led.

Whilst I wonder how to finish this story of my life, my favourite piece of music, Leo Delibes' 'The Flower Duet' sung by Katherine Jenkins, ebbs and flows in the room I choose to do my writing in. I will use the words of Hilaire Belloc as a bookend for a story about acutely vivid memories and very personal feelings, in a world which is changing and which I find increasingly difficult to fathom the fine detail of:

From quiet homes and first beginning,
Out to the undiscovered ends,
There's nothing worth the wear of winning,
But laughter and the love of friends

THE END

Acknowledgements

As it turns out I was right to suspect that my self-isolation during the start of the Covid-19 pandemic would provide my window of opportunity to finish the fragment of a book which I began working on many years ago. I knew I could never publish this book while either of my parents were still alive. They are both gone now and this is the right time to publish my story.

Locked down with my wife and two Old English Sheepdogs in a small bungalow in a tiny Yorkshire village required a sense of good judgement, in terms of not driving Bev quite bonkers. I am grateful to her for not making any attempt on my life while I was assembling the pieces of a story I have chosen to reveal at long last.

My special thanks go to my friends and associates who write for a living. I received good advice originally from Robert Gore Langton and much later from Bel Mooney. Most recently my publisher and editor Nick Awde was on hand with good solid advice and lots of encouragement.

Definitely deserving of sincere and heartfelt Thankyou's are a list of people. Some of the people listed below will perhaps wonder how they contributed to this book. Some provided encouragement and practical support. Others urged me to name and shame those who became flies in my life's ointment. I have identified a few people, but their actions only serve to emphasise firstly, that I must be a very poor judge of character and secondly that some folk must have minded me a lot more than I minded them.

Thank you to Julie Johnson, Jackie Hanson, Soraya Vivien, Joanne Speight, Barrie Lucas, Jennie Castell, Sue Smith and Tony Wayne.

Additional thanks should go to my agent Tracey Gunney and the resident genius figures in my life Adam Press and Martin Brown.

Photographic help came from Alan Hawes and from my own personal collection.

My family and my extended family all deserve to know the truth and what follows in this book, if nothing else, is both truthful and candid.

www.mark-ritchie.co.uk

Clockwise from top left: *My paternal grandfather Albert Webster Goodwin; my grandmother Mabel; my mother Mavis on receiving her diploma from the Royal College of Music in 1950; my father Frank Goodwin pictured in 1930 aged three.*

Top left: *newspaper reporter Bel Mooney pictured in 1979 with a group of miners from Nostell Colliery – I am pictured second from right.*
Centre left: *on my first wedding day with my sister Barbara and my parents in 1981.*
Centre right: *holding my daughter Michelle sitting alongside my friend John Law in 1990.*
Bottom: *visiting my old pal and roadie 'Throbber' aka Bob Mellor in hospital in Paralimni Cyprus 2003.*

Opposite: *Winning my first Clubland show business award in 1987.*

Top: *Complete with backing band in 1988.*
Left: *Actor Ian Ganderton my first ugly sister partner 2009 at the Parr Hall Theatre, Warrington.*

Opposite, clockwise from top left: *Four major talents... Jimmy Corrigan of Batley Variety fame; Siobhan Phillips (back then known as Shauna) who I consider to be the best female entertainer I ever worked with; comedian and pantomime legend Billy Pearce pictured way back in the mid 1970s; Tony Wayne, one of the few friends who has never let me down and a great cabaret artiste.*

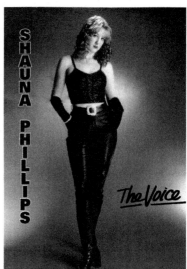

SHAUNA PHILLIPS

The Voice

BILLY PEARCE

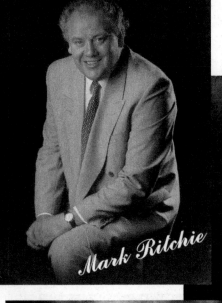

Various publicity photos from down the years taken by show business photographer Chris Meek.

Index

Also from Desert♥Hearts/Bennett & Bloom:

www.deserthearts.com
EMAIL US AT **info@deserthearts.com**
TO GO ON OUR MAILING LIST

*

WHAT NOW?
BEYOND DIVERSITY AND INCLUSION SERIES

EQUAL STAGES VOL 1:
Standing Up for Identity and Integrity in the Performing Arts

*

Singer-Songwriters, Volume 2: Beverley Craven, Judy Dyble,
Julia Fordham, Annie Haslam, Peggy Seeger, Judie Tzuke
Nick Awde

Singer-Songwriters, Volume 1: David Cousins, Arlo Guthrie,
Iain Matthews, Ralph McTell, Al Stewart, Richard Thompson
Nick Awde

Accidental Angel: Charity at Full Throttle *(out in 2021)*
Kate Copstick (of UK/Kenya charity Mama Biashara)

Electric Guitarists and Bassists, Volume 1 *(out in 2021)*
Nick Awde

Mellotron: The Machine and Musicians That Revolutionised Rock
Nick Awde

The Fifties Child: A Social History Through the Songs of
Barclay James Harvest
Alex Torres

The Vibrators: 21 Years of Punk Mania
Ian M. Carnochan (aka "Knox")

And on Piano . . . Nicky Hopkins: The Extraordinary Life of
Rock's Greatest Session Man
Julian Dawson

The Thin Book of Poems
Lach (Fortified Publishing/Desert Hearts)

The Wholly Viable: An Autoblography
Phil Kay

Freeing the Edinburgh Fringe: The Quest to Make Performers
Better Off by Charging the Public Nothing
Peter Buckley Hill

Critics: The Not So Dying Art of Theatre Criticism in the UK
(out in 2021)
Nick Awde

Solo: The Evolution of One-Person Theatre *(out in 2021)*
Nick Awde

The Happy Drunk
Bob Slayer

A Floristry of Palpitations
George Stanworth

The Big Bardaid Book
edited by Donna Daniels-Moss

Quaking in Me Stackheels: A Beginner's Guide to Surviving
Your First Public Performance
Paul Eccentric

The Commuter's Tale
Oliver Gozzard

The Little Big Woman Book
Llewella Gideon (illustrated by Nick Awde)

The Tattooing Arts of Tribal Women
Lars Krutak

Tattooed Mountain Women and Spoon Boxes of Daghestan:
Magic Medicine Symbols in Silk, Stone, Wood and Flesh
Robert Chenciner, Gabib Ismailov & Magomedkhan
Magomedkhanov

The Elfin Pedlar: A Cycle of Ballads On Traditional Themes
Freye Gray (illustrated by Ian M. Carnochan)

Andrew Lloyd Webber: The Musical
book, lyrics & music by Nick Awde

The Virgin Killers *(vol. 1 of The Public School Chronicles)*
Nick Awde

An Overseas Boy *(vol. 2 of The Public School Chronicles)*
Peter Lazard

Blood Confession *(vol. 3 of The Public School Chronicles)*
Nick Awde